IMPERIALISM

Social Classes

two essays by JOSEPH SCHUMPETER

Introduction by Bert Hoselitz
Translated by Heinz Norden

Meridian Books
THE WORLD PUBLISHING COMPANY
Cleveland and New York

A MERIDIAN BOOK

Published by The World Publishing Company
2231 West 110th Street, Cleveland 2, Ohio
First Meridian printing January 1955.
Seventh printing March 1964.
First published in Archiv für Sozialwissenschaft und
Sozialpolitik, Tübingen, Germany,
Vol. 46 (1919) and Vol. 57 (1927).
English translation first published by
Augustus M. Kelley, Inc., in 1951.
Printed in the United States of America.   7WP364

Contents

Introduction

When Joseph Schumpeter died, in January 1950, one month before his sixty-seventh birthday, he was generally acknowledged to have been one of the three or four greatest economists of his time. In the memorials which appeared in the months after his death his friends, students, and associates endeavored to answer three questions about his contribution to social science: which are Schumpeter's greatest and most lasting works; wherein consists the peculiar quality of his genius; and how can the apparently widely dissociated interests of the man be related to one another so as to form a coherent system of social thought?

It is impossible to answer these questions exhaustively in a few paragraphs, but a short survey of Schumpeter's life, his writings, and his actions, plans, and hopes go far to provide a fairly adequate picture of the nature and quality of his contribution to social science.

Not all of Schumpeter's adult life was spent in the quiet and peaceful environment of academic institutions. For a time he administered the estate of an Egyptian princess, was president of a private bank, in 1918 was a consultant of the Socialization Commission in Berlin, and for a few short months, in 1919, was Minister of Finance of Austria. From 1909 to 1920 Schumpeter held academic positions, first at Cernauti and then at Graz. Both were small universities in a provincial, narrow environment which was distasteful to him and from which he fled whenever his teaching obligations permitted. Even in 1925 when he was appointed to a professorship at Bonn, he was so heavily committed to writing articles on current economic topics for various magazines, that again he could not enjoy the calmness and serenity normally associated with academic life. Only when he came to Harvard in 1932 did he devote his full time to teaching and research. He consciously abstained from any attempt to exert a direct influence on practical affairs and, in 1943, turned to writing his last posthumously published book on the *History of Economic Analysis,* because, as he said in a letter, "it is simply the subject among all those at hand, that is farthest removed from current affairs."

In spite of the varied activities of his younger years, Schumpeter had produced three books by the time he was thirty-one. The first and third dealt with problems of economic theory and the history of economic ideas. They were solid and imaginative contributions to the science of economics, but they were not works which make history. His second book, *The Theory of Economic Development,* which appeared in 1912, established his reputation. This work contains his basic views on the dynamics of modern capitalism, and almost all his later scientific work—most of which was written more than two decades after the fertile outpouring of his youthful vision—constitutes an elaboration and refinement of the fundamental theories expostulated by a youthful man in his twenties.

The two essays reprinted in this volume belong to this group of writings. Imperialism had been subjected to a scientific study first by John A. Hobson, Rudolf Hilferding and Rosa Luxemburg. They all considered it an aspect of mature capitalism. What was more natural than that Schumpeter should attempt to throw further light on it and determine its relationship to the dynamics of capitalism as expounded in his system? The problem of class structure in modern society also was under dispute. Capitalism was based on slogans emphasizing the equality of all men. Yet, social classes and class differences continued to exist. Here were two problems whose full explanation went beyond purely economic analysis and which required sociological and historical depth for their full solution.

Far from being satisfied with explaining imperialism with reference to cycles of overproduction, the concentration of finance capital, or a struggle for markets or outlets for investment, as his predecessors had done, Schumpeter searched for a basically social explanation of imperialism. Instead of asking, what is imperialism? he asks, who are the imperialists? What groups in society form the spearhead of imperialist policies? How do these groups come into being? And what makes them disappear? Similarly in the case of social classes, he asks not what these classes are, but what function certain social structures perform under different economic and social conditions, and how the control of different values (i.e., objects of aspiration) determine differences in class structure.

Schumpeter's analysis of the sociology of imperialism and class structure is closely related to his analysis of economic growth. In each case he identifies a particular group, an elite, which under given historical and sociological conditions becomes the carrier of a movement. The carrier of economic development is the innovating entrepreneur. The carrier of imperialist ventures is the "machine of warriors, created by wars that required it, which now creates the wars it requires." The capitalistic elite is a group of peaceful businessmen whose main "exploits" are profit-making innovations. The imperialistic elite is an aristocracy whose chief reason for existence is the ever-renewed unleashing of aggressive wars.

The essay on social classes is a study of the connections between the ancient imperialisms and modern capitalist civilization in which aggressive war and imperialism has become an atavism. Schumpeter contrasts a social order in which the peak positions are held by an aristocracy, often with strong military leanings, to one in which the center of the stage is taken by a bourgeoisie led by a group of creative entrepreneurs. But the class structures and leadership patterns in an aristocratic and a bourgeois society differ because under each of the two systems different "socially necessary functions" need to be performed. As Schumpeter points out, this difference may be stated by saying that "the feudal master class was once—and the bourgeoisie was never —the supreme pinnacle of a uniformly constructed social pyramid. The feudal nobility was once—and the bourgeoisie was never—not only the sole possessor of physical power; it was physical power incarnate. . . . The nobility conquered the material complement to its position, while the bourgeoisie created this complement for itself."

These two essays form, in a very real sense, the capstone to Schumpeter's system. They were written in the interval between his fertile youth and the re-evaluation of his doctrines in his mature age. But although Schumpeter wrote (in addition to many articles) three full-sized books during his Harvard period, he never again discussed the problems of imperialism and social classes in his later work. Hence, we may regard these two essays as the final word he had to say on these subjects. His concern with the nature of capitalist dynamics demanded that he contrast it with socio-economic movements in pre-capitalist periods. Who took on leadership roles in society in the absence of the creative entrepreneurs? What were the conditions which brought forth these leaders, and why were they able to perform the "socially necessary functions" of their societies? In the essays on imperialism and on social classes the answers to these questions are provided. The process of capitalist development is not only set against a different process of feudalist social dynamics, but at the same time placed in its historical perspective.

Schumpeter's emphasis of the role of elite groups appears to place him among several other writers of the first two decades of this century who also developed "elitist" theories. Pareto had suggested such a theory, but later Robert Michels and, especially, Gaetano Mosca had developed this idea further. Other aspects of elitist thinking were developed by Max Weber in his discussion of forms of domination. Schumpeter was, of course, aware of these men and their works. But there are several significant differences between Schumpeter's theorizing and that of the Italian elitist school. Michels and Mosca applied their theories to the explanation of forms of government or existing social structures. These theories were either completely, or at least, comparatively static. In Schumpeter's reasoning the elite is the main force accounting for the dynamics of a system. In fact it is Schumpeter's emphasis on dynamics, on social *processes,* which distinguishes his work not only from that of most contemporary economists and sociologists, but also from his teachers in the Austrian school of economics.

Although schooled in the analysis of rigorous logical theorems of stationary economic states, Schumpeter was most impressed by two men who were the butt of attack by the members of the Austrian school, Leon Walras and Karl Marx. Walras impressed Schumpeter as an economist in whose system the mutual interaction of all parts upon each other were clearly recognized and explicitly stated. Marx exerted an influence upon him in that he was the last and most outspoken exponent of a line of theorizing in which the dynamism of capitalist society was stressed. However much Schumpeter disagreed with many of the detailed theories of Marx he always acknowledged his genius in recognizing capitalism as a stage in the development of human society and in emphasizing that only by studying its dynamics can one gain full understanding of its nature.

Schumpeter's main contribution to social theory consists then, above all, in having overcome the partial equilibrium analysis of the Austrian school of economics and replacing it by emphasis on general equilibrium; a general equilibrium, moreover, in which due attention is paid not merely to economic factors, but also to political and social forces. In addition it consists in his stressing the essential sterility of the static approach and the need to regard social phenomena as dynamic processes, whose most important dimension is the historical. This is confirmed by a statement Schumpeter made in his last work, the posthumously published *History of Economic Analysis.* Discussing the relation of statistics (economic measurement), economic theory, and economic history, and finding that all three are important for the progress of science, he concludes by saying, "I wish to state right now that, if starting my work in economics afresh, I were told that I could study only one of the three, but have my choice, it would be history I would choose." But the essays reprinted in this volume show that his conception of economic history was much wider than is common. The inclusion of all socially relevant phenomena and, as the essay on imperialism shows, the survey of all human historical experience were the material upon which Schumpeter's theories and insights are based. These essays, therefore, exhibit perhaps more clearly than any other of his works how true the designation was which his colleagues and friends gave him when he died: *Schumpeter, Social Scientist.* *

BERT HOSELITZ, 1955

* This is the title of a book, edited by S. E. Harris, containing 20 essays on the life and various aspects of the work of J. A. Schumpeter.

The Sociology of Imperialisms

THE PROBLEM

Our problem arises from the fact that aggressive attitudes on the part of states—or of such earlier organizational structures as history may record—can be explained, directly and unequivocally, only in part by the real and concrete interests of the people. Examples will best illustrate what we mean. When two tribes come into conflict over essential salt deposits or hunting grounds; or when a state, hemmed in on all sides by customs and communication barriers, resorts to aggression in order to gain access to the sea, we have a case in which aggression is explained by interests. It is true that there are many methodological difficulties in speaking of the interests of a people as such. Here, however, reference to "concrete" interests explains everything that would seem to stand in need of explanation. A concrete interest need not be economic in character. When a state resorts to aggression in order to unite its citizens politically, as was the case with Piedmont in 1848 and 1859, this likewise betokens a real, concrete interest, explaining its conduct. The interest, moreover, need not necessarily extend to the *entire* population of the state. When a planter aristocracy prevails upon its government to seize some foreign base of operations for the slave

3

trade, this too is explained by a real, concrete interest. The interest that actually explains a warlike act need not, finally, be openly admitted—or of the kind that *can* be openly admitted; it need not, to use our own term, be an *avowed* interest. Such cases nevertheless come under the present heading, if the concrete interests of a sufficiently powerful class are accessible to scientific consideration. There are, on the other hand, certain cases that do *not* belong here, such as that of a group of people who contrive to have a declaration of war issued because they gain financially from the waging of war, or because they need a war as a diversion from domestic political difficulties. Here there is no concrete interest, in the sense that applies to the aforementioned cases. True, there must be *some* concrete interest. There must be a reason for the declaration of war. But that *reason* is not the *cause*. The true cause, of course, must also lie in an interest. But that interest is not in the concrete war aims. It is not a question of the advantages offered by the attainment of those aims, but of an interest in the waging of war as such. The questions that then arise are how the people came to acquire such a generally belligerent disposition and why they happened to choose this particular occasion for war. Thus mere reference to a concrete interest is satisfactory under only three conditions: In the first place, such a concrete interest *must be present*, in the sense that has now been made clear —an interest which the observer can grasp as such, of course taking into account the social structure, mentality, and situation of the people in question. In the second place, the conduct of the state which is under study must be calculated to *promote* this interest, with the sum total of predictable sacrifices and risks in some proportion to the anticipated gains. In the third place, it must be possible to *prove* that this interest, whether avowed or not, is actually the *political driving force* behind the action.

In the individual case it may often become difficult to establish whether these conditions obtain. The fabric of social interests is so closely woven that scarcely ever can there be any action on the part of a state that is not in keeping with the concrete interest of someone, an interest to which that action can be reduced without manifest absurdity. To this must be added the belief, inculcated into the people, especially in the present age, that concrete interests of the people dictate the behavior of the state and that concrete advantages for all classes are to be expected. Government policies are always officially justified in this way, and often, without the slightest doubt, in perfect good faith. Finally, current fallacies, especially of an economic character, may serve to create the semblance of an adequate, concrete interest in the mind of the people—and occasionally even in the mind of the scientific observer, especially the historian. In such cases the true background is laid bare only by inquiry into the manner in which the people came to their belief. But the individual case does not concern us. We are concerned only with the fact, which is beyond doubt, that the three above-mentioned conditions are frequently not fulfilled. Whenever such is the case, a problem arises. And among the problems of this nature is the problem of imperialism.

No one calls it imperialism when a state, no matter how brutally and vigorously, pursues concrete interests of its own; and when it can be expected to abandon its aggressive attitude as soon as it has attained what it was after. The word "imperialism" has been abused as a slogan to the point where it threatens to lose all meaning, but up to this point our definition is quite in keeping with common usage, even in the press. For whenever the word imperialism is used, there is always the implication—whether sincere or not—of an aggressiveness, the true reasons for which do not lie in the aims which are temporarily being pursued; of an aggressiveness that is only kindled anew by each success; of an aggressiveness for its own sake, as reflected in such terms as "hegemony," "world dominion," and so forth. And history, in truth, shows us nations and classes—most nations furnish an example at some time or other—that seek expansion for the sake of expanding, war for the sake of fighting, victory for the sake of winning, dominion for the sake of ruling. This determination cannot be explained by any of the pretexts that bring it into action, by any of the aims for which it seems to be struggling at the time. It confronts us, independent of all concrete purpose or occasion, as an enduring disposition, seizing upon one opportunity as eagerly as the next. It shines through all the arguments put forward on behalf of present aims. It values conquest not so much on account of the immediate advantages—advantages that more often than not are more than dubious, or that are heedlessly cast away with the same frequency—as because it *is* conquest, success, action. Here the theory of concrete interest in our sense fails. What needs to be explained is how the will to victory itself came into being.

Expansion for its own sake always requires, among other things, concrete objects if it is to reach the action stage and maintain itself, but this does not constitute its meaning. Such expansion is in a sense its own "object," and the truth is that it has no adequate object beyond itself. Let us therefore, in the absence of a better term, call it "objectless." It follows for that very reason that, just as such expansion cannot be explained by concrete interest, so too it is never satisfied by the fulfillment of a concrete interest, as would be the case if fulfillment were the motive, and the struggle for it merely a necessary evil—a counterargument, in fact. Hence the tendency of such expansion to transcend all bounds and tangible limits, to the point of utter exhaustion. This, then, is our definition: imperialism is the objectless disposition on the part of a state to unlimited forcible expansion.

Now it may be possible, in the final analysis, to give an "economic explanation" for this phenomenon, to end up with economic factors. Two different points present themselves in this connection: First, an attempt can be made, following the basic idea of the economic interpretation of history, to derive imperialist tendencies from the economic-structural influences that shape life in general and from the relations of production. I should like to emphasize that I do not doubt in the least that this powerful instrument of analysis will stand up here in the same sense that it has with other, similar phenomena—if only it is kept in mind that customary modes of political thought and feeling in a given age can never be mere "reflexes" of, or counterparts to, the production situation of that age. Because of the persistence of such habits, they will always, to a considerable degree, be dominated by the production context of past ages. Again, the attempt may be made to reduce imperialist phenomena to economic class *interests* of the age in question. This is precisely what neo-Marxist theory does. Briefly, it views imperialism simply as the reflex of the interests of the capitalist upper stratum, at a given stage of capitalist development. Beyond doubt this is by far the most serious contribution toward a solution of our problem. Certainly there is much truth in it. We shall deal with this theory later. But let us emphasize even here that it does not, of logical necessity, follow from the economic interpretation of history. It may be discarded without coming into conflict with that interpretation; indeed, without even departing from its premises. It is the treatment of this factor that constitutes the contribution of the present inquiry into the sociology of the *Zeitgeist*.[1]

Our method of investigation is simple: we propose to analyze the birth and life of imperialism by means of historical examples which I regard as typical. A common basic trait emerges in every case, making a single sociological problem of imperialism in all ages, though there are substantial differences among the individual cases. Hence the plural, "imperialisms," in the title.

IMPERIALISM AS A CATCH PHRASE

An example will suffice. After the split over the question of repealing the Corn Laws in the year 1846, the Conservative Party in England, reconstituted around Stanley, Bentinck, and Disraeli, was in an extremely difficult situation. During long years of unbroken dominance, ever since the Napoleonic wars, it had at bottom lacked even a single positive plank in its platform. Its entire program may be summarized in the word "No!" [1] Its best heads soon recognized that they could get away with such a policy in wartime, but not under normal circumstances. Canning was the first to grasp this truth, and it was he who created that highest type of Conservative policy which consists in refusing to shrink from the great necessities of the day, and instead seizes upon them realistically and constructs Conservative successes on what would otherwise have become Conservative defeats. One of his two great accomplishments was his struggle for national freedom throughout the world—a struggle that created a background of international good will that was to mean so much in the future; the Catholic emancipation was the other. When Peel moved up to leadership, he could not follow the same policy, for his followers would have rebelled. He chose to fight against electoral reform, which played into the hands of the Whigs under Lord Grey and helped them to their long rule. Yet at the height of his power (1842-1846) Peel did conduct himself in the spirit of Canning. He made the cause of free trade his own. The great undertaking succeeded—an accomplishment I have always regarded as the greatest of its kind in the history of domestic politics. Its fruits were a sharp rise in prosperity, sustained social peace, sound foreign relations. But the Conservative Party was wrecked in the process. Those who remained loyal to Peel—the Peelites—first formed a special group, only to be absorbed by the legions of Liberalism later on. Those who seceded formed the new Conservative Party, for the time being essentially agrarian in character. But they lacked a platform that would have attracted a majority, a banner to be flung to the breezes of popular favor, a leader whom they trusted. That was shown after the death of Lord George Bentinck, who at least had been a convinced partisan of the Corn Laws; and it was shown especially in 1852 when the chances of the parliamentary game put Stanley (by then Lord Derby) and Disraeli in the saddle. To strengthen their minority—they could not hope for a majority—they dissolved Parliament. But in the ensuing election campaign they were so unsure of their cause that their opponents were able to claim with some justification that Derby candidates were protectionist in rural districts and free trade in urban ones. It could scarcely have been otherwise, for it was not hard to see that a return to the Corn Laws was out of the question, while the Conservative Party had nothing else to offer to the hard core of its followers. Failure was inevitable under such circumstances, nor was it long delayed. Thus when Disraeli picked up the reins a second time, once again with a minority (1858-1859), he ventured along a different course. He usurped the battle cry of electoral reform. This was a plausible policy from the Conservative point of view. An extension of the franchise was bound to give a voice to population segments that, for the time being at least, were more susceptible to Conservative arguments than the bourgeoisie which did not begin to swing over to the Conservative side until the seventies. At first Disraeli failed, but in 1866-1867 he succeeded all the better. Again in the minority, facing the latent hostility of his own people, reviled as no English statesman had been since Bute and North, beset with problems on every side, he yet revolutionized the electoral law—an unparalleled triumph of political genius. Disraeli fell, but in the midst of disaster the essence of victory was his. True, it was Gladstone's hour. All the forces and voices of victory fought for him. But as early as 1873 it was plain that the meteoric career of his first cabinet—or his second, if he be counted the actual head of Russell's cabinet—was drawing to a close. Reform legislation always brings in its wake a renascence of conservative sentiment. The Conservative election success of 1874 was more and more clearly foreshadowed. And what program did Disraeli, the Conservative leader, have to offer? The people did not ask for much in a positive way. They wanted a breathing space. Criticism of Gladstone's acts was highly rewarding under the circumstances. Yet some positive policy had to be offered. What would it be?

The Conservative leader spoke of social reform. Actually he was only reverting to Conservative traditions (Ashley) which he himself had helped to shape in earlier years. Besides, such a policy might split off a few radicals from Gladstone's camp. A certain kinship between the Conservatives and the radicals was of long standing—did not, in fact, cease, until the radicals had got the better of the Whigs within the Liberal Party. But the situation was unfavorable for "Tory democracy." For the moment, Gladstone had done more than enough in this field. The slogans were shopworn. There was prosperity. The working people turned every official trip of Gladstone's into a triumphal procession. No, there was little capital to be made on that score. It was no better with the Irish question—the cause of the Ulstermen and the High Church. In this predicament Disraeli struck a new note. The election campaign of 1874—or, to fix the date exactly, Disraeli's speech in the Crystal Palace in 1872—marked the birth of imperialism as the catch phrase of domestic policy.

It was put in the form of "Imperial Federation." The colonies—of which Disraeli in 1852 had written: "These wretched colonies . . . are a millstone round our necks" (Malmesbury, *Memoirs of an Ex-Minister,* p. 343)—these same colonies were to become autonomous members in a unified empire. This empire was to form a customs union. The free soil of the colonies was to remain reserved for Englishmen. A uniform defense system was to be created. The whole structure was to be crowned by a central representative organ in London, creating a closer, living connection between the imperial government and the colonies. The appeal to national sentiment, the battle cry against "Liberal" cosmopolitanism, already emerged sharply, just as they did later on in the agitation sponsored by Chamberlain, on whom fell Disraeli's mantle. Of itself the plan showed no inherent tendency to reach out beyond the "Empire," and "the Preservation of the Empire" was and is a good description of it. If we nevertheless include the "Imperial Federation" plan under the heading of imperialism, this is because its protective tariff, its militarist sentiments, its ideology of a unified

"Greater Britain" all foreshadowed vague aggressive trends that would have emerged soon enough if the plan had ever passed from the sphere of the slogan into the realm of actual policy.

That it was not without value as a slogan is shown by the very fact that a man of Chamberlain's political instinct took it up—characteristically enough in another period, when effective Conservative rallying cries were at a premium. Indeed, it never vanished again, becoming a stock weapon in the political arsenal of English Conservatism, usurped even by many Liberals. As early as the nineties it meant a great deal to the youth of Oxford and Cambridge. It played a leading part in the Conservative press and at Conservative rallies. Commercial advertising grew very fond of employing its emblems—which explains why it was so conspicuous to foreign (and usually superficial) observers, and why there was so much discussion in the foreign press about "British Imperialism," a topic, moreover, that was most welcome to many political parties on the Continent. This success is readily explained. In the first place, the plan had much to offer to a whole series of special interests—primarily a protective tariff and the prospect of lucrative opportunities for exploitation, inaccessible to industry under a system of free trade. Here was the opportunity to smother consumer resistance in a flood of patriotic enthusiasm. Later on, this advantage weighed all the more heavily in the balance, for certain English industries were beginning to grow quite sensitive to the dumping tactics employed by German and American exporters. Of equal importance was the fact that such a plan was calculated to divert the attention of the people from social problems at home. But the main thing, before which all arguments stemming from calculating self-interest must recede into the background, was the unfailing power of the appeal to national sentiment. No other appeal is as effective, except at a time when the people happen to be caught in the midst of flaming social struggle. All other appeals are rooted in interests that must be grasped by reason. This one alone arouses the dark powers of the subconscious, calls into play instincts that carry over from the life habits of the dim past. Driven out everywhere else, the irrational seeks refuge in nationalism—the irrational which consists of belligerence, the need to hate, a goodly quota of inchoate idealism, the most naive (and hence also the most unrestrained) egotism. This is precisely what constitutes the impact of nationalism. It satisfies the need for surrender to a concrete and familiar superpersonal cause, the need for self-glorification and violent self-assertion. Whenever a vacuum arises in the mind of a people —as happens especially after exhausting social agitation, or after a war—the nationalist element comes to the fore. The idea of "Imperial Federation" gave form and direction to these trends in England. It was, in truth, a fascinating vision which was unfolded before the provincial mind. An additional factor was a vague faith in the advantages of colonial possessions, preferably to be exploited to the exclusion of all foreigners. Here we see ancient notions still at work. Once upon a time it had been feasible to treat colonies in the way that highwaymen treat their victims, and the possession of colonies unquestionably brought advantages. Trade had been possible only under immediate military protection and there could be no question that military bases were necessary.[2] It is because of the survival of such arguments that colonialism is not yet dead, even in England today, though only in exceptional circumstances do colonies under free trade become objects of exploitation in a sense different from that in which independent countries can be exploited. And finally, there is the instinctive urge to domination. Objectively, the man in the street derives little enough satisfaction even from modern English colonial policy, but he does take pleasure in the idea, much as a card player vicariously satisfies his primitive aggressive instincts. At the time of the Boer War there was not a beggar in London who did not speak of "our" rebellious subjects. These circumstances, in all their melancholy irony, are serious factors in politics. They eliminate many courses of action that alone seem reasonable to the leaders. Here is an example: In 1815 the Ionian Islands became an English protectorate, not to be surrendered until

1863. Long before then, however, one foreign secretary after another had realized that this possession was meaningless and untenable—not in the absolute sense, but simply because no reasonable person in England would have approved of the smallest sacrifice on its behalf. Nevertheless, none dared surrender it, for it was clear that this would have appeared as a loss and a defeat, chalked up against the cabinet in question. The only thing to do was to insist that Corfu was a military base of the highest importance which must be retained. Now, during his first term as head of the government, Gladstone had frequently made concessions—to Russia, to America, to others. At bottom everyone was glad that he had made them. Yet an uncomfortable feeling persisted, together with the occasion for much speech-making about national power and glory. The political genius who headed the opposition party saw all this—and *spoke* accordingly.

That this imperialism is no more than a phrase is seen from the fact that Disraeli *spoke,* but did not *act.* But this alone is not convincing. After all, he might have lacked the opportunity to act. The crucial factor is that he *did* have the opportunity. He had a majority. He was master of his people as only an English prime minister can be. The time was auspicious. The people had lost patience with Gladstone's peace-loving nature. Disraeli owed his success in part to the slogan we have been discussing. Yet he did not even try to follow through. He took not a single step in that direction. He scarcely even mentioned it in his speeches, once it had served his purpose. His foreign policy moved wholly within the framework of Conservative tradition. For this reason it was pro-Austrian and pro-Turkish. The notion that the integrity of Turkey was in the English interest was still alive, not yet overthrown by the power of Gladstone's Midlothian speeches which were to change public opinion on this point and later, under Salisbury, invade even the Conservative credo. Hence the new Earl of Beaconsfield supported Turkey, hence he tore up the Treaty of San Stefano. Yet even this, and the capture of Cyprus, were of no avail. A tide of public indignation toppled his rule soon afterward.[3]

We can see that Beaconsfield was quite right in not taking a single step in the direction of practical imperialism and that his policy was based on good sense. The masses of the British electorate would never have sanctioned an imperialist policy, would never have made sacrifices for it. As a toy, as a political arabesque, they accepted imperialism, just so long as no one tried it in earnest. This is seen conclusively when the fate of Chamberlain's agitation is traced. Chamberlain was unquestionably serious. A man of great talent, he rallied every ounce of personal and political power, marshaled tremendous resources, organized all the interests that stood to gain, employed a consummate propaganda technique—all this to the limits of the possible. Yet England rejected him, turning over the reins to the opposition by an overwhelming majority. It condemned the Boer War, did everything in its power to "undo" it, proving that it was merely a chance aberration from the general trend.[4] So complete was the defeat of imperialism that the Conservatives under Bonar Law, in order to achieve some degree of political rehabilitation, had to strike from their program the tariffs on food imports, necessarily the basis for any policy of colonial preference.

The rejection of imperialism meant the rejection of all the interests and arguments on which the movement was based. The elements that were decisive for the formation of political will power—above all the radicals and gradually the labor representatives as well—showed little enthusiasm for the ideology of world empire. They were much more inclined to give credence to the Disraeli of 1852, who had compared colonies to millstones, than to the Disraeli of 1874, to the Chamberlain of the eighties rather than the Chamberlain of 1903. They showed not the least desire to make presents to agriculture, whether from national or other pretexts, at the expense of the general welfare. They were far too well versed in the free-trade argument—and this applies to the very lowest layers of the English electorate—to believe the gloomy prophecies of the "yellow press," which insisted that free trade was sacrificing to current consumer interests employment opportunities and the very roots of material welfare.

After all, the rise of British export trade after 1900 belied this argument as plainly as could be. Nor had they any sympathy for military splendor and adventures in foreign policy. The whole struggle served only to demonstrate the utter impotence of jingoism. The question of "objective interest" —that is, whether and to what extent there is an economic interest in a policy of imperialism—remains to be discussed.[5] Here we are concerned only with those political notions that have proved effective—whether they were false or true.

What effect the present war will have in this respect remains to be seen. For our purposes what has still to be shown is how this anti-imperialist sentiment—and especially anti-imperialism in practice—developed in England. In the distant past England did have imperialist tendencies, just as most other nations did. The process that concerns us now begins with the moment when the struggle between the people and the crown ended differently in England from the way it did on the Continent—namely, with the victory of the people. Under the Tudors and Stuarts the absolute monarchy developed in England much as it did at the same time on the Continent. Specifically, the British Crown also succeeded in winning over part of the nobility, the "cavaliers," who subsequently sided with it against the "roundheads" and who, but for the outcome of the battles of Naseby and Marston Moor, would surely have become a military palace guard.[6] Presumably England, too, would then have seen the rise of an arbitrary military absolutism, and the same tendencies which we shall discover elsewhere would have led to continual wars of aggression there too. That is why the defeat of the king and his party represent so decisive a juncture for our subject, a break in continuity. For by way of Charles I's scaffold, of Cromwell, of the Restoration, and of the events of 1688, the way led to freedom—at first, it is true, to the freedom of only one class, even to the dominance of a privileged class. But this was a class that could maintain its position only because—and so long as—it assumed leadership of those segments of the population which counted in politics—the urban population (even those without the franchise had ways of making themselves felt), yeomen, farmers, clerics, and "intellectuals." It was a class, in other words, that very soon had to learn how to behave like a candidate for public office. It might on occasion depart from such an attitude, but each time it paid dearly. The crown might seek to intervene, but each time such an effort ended in a more or less humiliating setback. The electorate may have been very narrowly circumscribed, but the ruling class depended on it—and even more on public opinion—much as on the Continent it was dependent on the monarch. And that made a great difference. In particular, it turned foreign policy into something altogether different from what it was on the Continent. The entire motivation of continental monarchial policy gave way to something different. This does not mean that a policy made by the monarch and his courtiers was impossible—it merely became one of many factors. It had to curry favor, was strictly controlled, and, if it transcended the formulated will of a party that commanded a sufficiently powerful segment of the public, always succumbed in the end to a storm which no minister's nerves could stand up to.[7] From that time on, secret diplomacy in England survived only in the literal sense—in the sense that a circle of professionals rallied around the man responsible for foreign policy, a circle that was susceptible to irresponsible influences of various kinds and often, in ways that were obscure to the public, acted in a manner that would never have been approved, had the true facts of the matter become known. But there was no secret diplomacy in the deeper sense, no circle that was able, in secret, to determine the whole course of foreign policy, as the councilors of a continental sovereign could. As soon as the results of their actions came to light, British statesmen were subject to the verdict of Parliament and of public opinion, which were able to mete out punishment where they did not approve. This made foreign policy part and parcel of partisan politics, the concern of the people who mattered in a political sense.

It is important to grasp the full implications of these facts. The parties succeeded each other in power, and each one had different aims and policies. One might declare war and wage it victoriously, only to be brought down by the other, which might at once conclude peace and surrender some of the gains which had been won. One might enter into alliances which the other would dissolve. One might bask in national glory, while the other would calculate the costs to the people. In this way England, since 1688, has lacked an unbroken, planned political line. If there was the appearance of such a thing, it was only the consequence of the fact that certain iron necessities prevailed in the face of all deliberate efforts to escape them; in part, also, the consequence of biased interpretation. True, even the policies of continental states were not necessarily governed by strict logic. But in the case of the advisers of such sovereigns the driving forces, interests, traditions, and motivations behind policies were firmly fixed. They brought a certain consistency to the whole picture, while in England it was precisely the driving forces and interests that so frequently alternated. There was only one point on which the parties were always in agreement. This was to prevent the rise of a professional army; and when that rise had become unavoidable, to keep the army as small as possible and prevent it from growing into a separate occupational estate with independent power and distinct interests. This element always worked in the same direction: it served to eliminate any factor that might have continually pressed for aggression.

We see this even at the outset of the new era. A peace party as such arose at once, and has persisted ever since, to act as a brake on any policy of aggression. At first it consisted of the Tories, the clerical party, the small landowners, the yeomen, the farmers. All of them wanted to go riding and hunting, or till the soil, in peace. They looked on all war as sheer Whig deviltry. European policies and overseas struggles were matters of supreme indifference to them, which was not at all true of the tax burden which at that time fell primarily on them.

The Whigs, for their part, were all the more belligerent. They were the party of the great lords on the one hand, and

the City on the other. For, in the first place, colonial possessions at that time really meant more than they do today. War
was then still something it has no longer been since about
the time of the French Revolution—good business. Again—
and this is something that is overlooked unbelievably often
—it behooved the Whigs to defend the newly won freedom
—and with it their own position—against unquestionable
aggressive intentions on the part of France. Finally, it
was up to them to hold those national positions throughout
the world that had been captured by their individual co-
nationals rather than by the state as such.

These last two factors make it appear doubtful whether it
is proper to speak of eighteenth-century English imperialism
in our sense. At the very least, it would be a very special
imperialism, quite different from the continental brand. As
in the case of Spain, England at first merely *defended* itself
against France. True, the defense was so successful that it
passed over into conquest. And it is also true that appetite
appeared in the eating. The first of our three factors certainly
supported any and every predisposition toward war. The
wars of that period were commercial wars, *among other
things,* but to describe them *only* as commercial wars is
simply historically untrue—for the French as well as the
English side of the question. It is noteworthy, furthermore,
that it was not the English *state* that conquered the colonial
empire. Usually the state intervened in a protective capacity
—generally with extreme reluctance and under duress—only
when a colony was already in existence. More than that, it
cannot even be said that it was "the people" who conquered
the whole empire, that the leading men embarked on conquest to the plaudits of the public. The conquerors were of
an altogether different stripe—adventurers who were unable
to find a solid footing at home, or men driven into exile. In
the latter case there was the simple necessity for finding a
new home. In the former it was a question of elements who,
on the Continent, would have joined the armies of the sovereigns and vented their belligerent instincts on their own
people or on some other European state. Since England had

no sovereign who could have hired or paid them, they ventured out into the world and waged war on their own—"private imperialists," as it were. But the people refused to go along. No one was more unpopular than the slave trader, or the "nabob" who returned with his pockets full of plundered gold. Only with great effort could such a man secure social position. The public attitude toward him was similar to the reaction toward "war profiteers" nowadays. As often as not, he was haled into court. But of course it is true that every war creates groups interested in that war. Armaments always create a predisposition toward war. And every war is father to another war.

England's attitude toward revolutionary France, like that of the continental states, was doubtless in part determined by lust for booty. But that attitude is seen in its true light only when it is compared with the character of the rule of the younger Pitt before the French Revolution. That character was most clearly expressed in the French Treaty of 1786. Pitt was a typical minister of peace. It was to peace, free trade, and the dissolution of mercantilism that England aspired under his leadership. Thus the English attitude toward the France of the Revolution and of Napoleon must be understood as a departure from the prior trend rather than as a step along that line of evolution.[8] The period that followed showed that the Napoleonic wars were but an interlude. At first, England followed in the wake of the Holy Alliance,[9] which was anything but imperialist. And the earliest stirrings of an independent policy—in Huskisson's campaign for free trade—were linked to Pitt's prerevolutionary principles. As for Canning, his Greek policy struck a new note which, as we can see today, was intimately linked with free-trade trends and which may be summarized in the single word: *anti-imperialism*.

The two great parties, Tories and Whigs, maintained the foreign policy positions that have been indicated about as long as they did their names, to about 1840. Even the last typical Whig foreign ministers (and prime ministers), Palmerston and Russell, were "activist" in character. Yet all that was really left to them was the old bias, for the actual direction of their "activism" was forced on them by changed circumstances. They intervened everywhere in the world, generally in a challenging tone, ready to throw out military threats. They defended even unimportant interests with aggressive vigor—the classic expression of this aspect of their policy is Lord Palmerston's *Civis Romanus* speech of 1850. Toward the colonies, they stressed the claim of the central power to submission. But the people compelled them, first, to give a wide berth to what is called "economic imperialism"—a matter we have yet to discuss. Both were or became free traders. Both fought against the slave labor. And the people compelled them, second, to act on behalf of national liberation and against oppression, misgovernment, and imperialism, whenever they transcended England's immediate sphere of interests. This they did, and thus these men, whose political genealogy certainly had its roots elsewhere, became advocates of national, political, and religious self-determination throughout the world.[10] It has become the custom to describe this as "hypocrisy." But we are not at all concerned with the individual motives of these two statesmen. Suppose they were hypocrites, in the subjective sense —though it is far from easy for anyone to pretend a whole life long. Suppose this policy was mainly determined by the realization that it would open up to England inexhaustible resources of power and sympathy—which was what actually happened. The point that concerns us is that their policy was the only one that was tenable in England, in the parliamentary sense, that it was a means for winning political victories at home. It follows that it must have been in accord with the true intentions of the "important people" and, beyond them, of the masses. And the masses are never hypocritical.

It is not difficult to find an explanation. Moral progress is here directly linked with the "conditions of production." The sociological meaning of the process lies in the relationship between this policy and contemporary free-trade trends. The interests of trade and everyday life in England had turned pacifist, and the process of social restratification that marked the Industrial Revolution brought these interests to the fore. It was a process that only now bore all of its political fruits, and the interests it carried to the top were those of industry, in contradistinction to those of the trade monopolists of the seventeenth and eighteenth centuries. The principles of free trade were now carried to victory by Sir Robert Peel's Conservatives and later accepted even by Disraeli's new party. This was the original occasion for that "regrouping" of forces behind the political parties that ultimately led the industrial-capitalist class (including the banking fraternity) and almost the entire high aristocracy into the Conservative camp, while Liberalism became more and more the party of the Nonconformists and intellectuals—except for most clerics and lawyers—and, for a time, of working-class interests as well. And it was the great ministry of Sir Robert Peel that inaugurated, with complete logic, the policy that, despite many relapses into former habits, has become more and more the policy of England; a policy adopted by the Liberal Party through the instrumentality of Gladstone and under the influence of the rising power of the radicals, while the opposing trends gathered under the Conservative banner; a policy that for the first time seriously applied the full consequences of free trade,[11] emancipating itself from the old notions of the tasks of diplomacy; a policy that may be summarized under the following principles: never to intervene, unless vital interests are gravely and immediately threatened; never to be concerned about the "balance of power" on the Continent; not to arm for war; to reduce, by means of understandings, those areas of friction with other spheres of interest that were particularly extensive because of the lack of planning in the global structure of empire; to relieve tension and conflict by appropriate yielding, to the point where the remaining British sphere would be at least halfway tenable. That policy encountered immense difficulties in the acquired habits of political thought and emotional reaction, in concrete situations taken over from earlier times, in individual interests, and above all in the fact that championing it in Parliament in each case was generally a thankless task, offering ready-made points of attack to the opposition. Nevertheless, in spite of all aberrations, it prevailed time and again, because it was in accord with the objective interests of the politically important segments of the population, including, after the eighties, above all the industrial workers. From Peel to Lansdowne and Grey, it continually reasserted itself, like the level of a storm-tossed ocean.

We see therefore that the imperialist wave that in recent decades has been beating against the mainland of social evolution in England did not rise from the true depths of that evolution but was rather a temporary reaction of political sentiment and of threatened individual interests. Aggressive nationalism (to which we shall revert), the instincts of dominance and war derived from the distant past and alive down to the present—such things do not die overnight. From time to time they seek to come into their own, all the more vigorously when they find only dwindling gratifications within the social community. But where, as in England, there is a lack of sufficiently powerful interests with which those trends might ally themselves, an absence of warlike structural elements in the social organization, there they are condemned to political impotence. War may call them back to life, even lead to a more closely knit organization of the country, one that appears more aggressive toward the outside. But it cannot alter the basis of social and political structure. Even in England imperialism will remain a plaything of politics for a long time to come. But in terms of *practical* politics, there is no room left for it there—except possibly as a means for defense—nor any support among the real powers behind the policies of the day.[12]

IMPERIALISM IN PRACTICE

What imperialism looks like when it is not mere words, and what problems it offers, can best be illustrated by examples from antiquity. We shall select the Egyptian, Assyrian, and Persian empires and later add certain examples from a more recent period of history. We shall find characteristic differences among them, as well as one basic trait common to all, even the most modern brand of imperialism —a trait which for that reason alone cannot very well be the product of modern economic evolution.

The case of Egypt, down to the Persian occupation, is particularly instructive, because here we see the imperialist trend toward expansion actually in the making. The Egyptians of the "Old" and "Middle" Empires—down to the Hyksos invasion—were a nation of peasants. The soil was the property of a hereditary, latifundian nobility which let it out to the peasants and which ruled in the political sense as well. This fundamental fact found organizational expression in a "regional" feudalism, an institution that was for the most part hereditary, rooted in real property, and, especially during the Middle Empire, quite independent of the crown. This social structure bore all the outward marks of force, yet it lacked any inherent tendency toward violent and unlimited expansion. The external situation ruled out such a trend; for the country, while easy to defend, was quite unsuitable as a base for a policy of conquest in the grand manner. Nor was it demanded by economic requirements—and indeed, no trace of such a policy is apparent. Throughout the period of the "Old" Empire of Memphis we learn of but one warlike undertaking (except for unimportant fighting on the Sinai peninsula). This was the campaigns in southern Syria under the Sixth Dynasty. In the "Middle" Empire of Thebes things were not quite so peaceful; still, fighting revolved essentially only about the defense of the frontiers. The single conquest was Nubia (under Amenemhat I and Usertesen III).

Things changed only after the expulsion of the Hyksos (whom Manetho counts as the Fifteenth and Sixteenth Dynasties), in the "New" Empire. The immediate successors of the liberator, Aahmes I, already conquered upper Cush to the third cataract and then reached farther into Asia. They grew more and more aggressive, and campaign followed campaign, without the slightest concrete cause. Dhutmes III and Amenhotep III were conquerors, pure and simple. In the end Egyptian rule reached to the Amanes and beyond the Euphrates. Following a reversal under the Nineteenth and Twentieth Dynasties, this policy was resumed, and after the Assyrian invasion (662) and the liberation by Psamtik I, Egypt, reunited under Necho II, again passed over to the attack, until the Battle of Karkamish (604) put an end to its Asiatic undertakings. Why did all this happen?

The facts enable us to diagnose the case. The war of liberation from the Hyksos, lasting a century and a half, had "militarized" Egypt. A class of professional soldiers had come into being, replacing the old peasant militia and technically far superior to it, owing to the employment of battle chariots, introduced, like the horse, by the Bedouin Hyksos. The support of that class enabled the victorious kings, as early as Aahmes I, to reorganize the empire centrally and to suppress the regional feudal lords and the large, aristocratic landowners—or at least to reduce their importance. We hear little about them in the "New" Empire. The crown thus carried out a social revolution; it became the ruling power, together with the new military and hierarchical aristocracy and, to an increasing degree, foreign mercenaries as well. This new social and political organization was essentially a war machine. It was motivated by warlike instincts and interests. Only in war could it find an outlet and maintain its domestic position. Without continual passages at arms it would necessarily have collapsed. Its external orientation was war, and war alone. Thus war became the normal condition, alone conducive to the well-being of the organs of the body social that now existed. To take the field was a matter of course, the reasons for doing so were of subordinate importance. *Created by wars that required it, the machine now created the wars it required.* A will for broad conquest without tangible limits, for the capture of positions that were manifestly untenable—this was typical imperialism.

The case of the Persians is distinct from that of the Egyptians in that the former appear as a "warrior nation" from the very outset. What does that term mean? Manifestly, a nation whose social structure is oriented toward the military function, that does not need to be readjusted to that function by the power of the crown and a new warrior class, added at some time to the previously existing classes; a nation where the politically important classes—but not necessarily *all* the classes—view warfare as their main profession, are professional soldiers, do not need to be specially trained as such. The crucial point is *not* the mere capacity or inclination to resort to arms when the need arises. The landlords and even the peasants of Egypt were originally no strangers to the profession of arms. But it was *not* their profession as such. They took up arms much as the modern "civilian" joins the army—when they had to. Their lives were centered in the private rather than the military sphere. War was a nuisance—an abnormal emergency. What *is* the crucial point is that in a warrior nation war is never regarded as an emergency interfering with private life; but, on the contrary, that life and vocation are fully realized *only* in war. In a warrior nation the social community is a war community. Individuals are never absorbed into the private sphere. There is always an excess of energy, finding its natural complement in war. The will to war and violent expansion rises directly from the people—though this term is here not necessarily used in the democratic sense, as we shall see later.

Hence the term "people's imperialism," which today is unquestionably nonsense, is in good standing when applied to a warrior nation.

The Persians offer a good example of such a warrior nation. True, even *their* organization did not emerge fullfledged until the conquest of Elam (second half of the sixth century). True, even with *them* the crown grew powerful only in the ensuing period of triumphs. And, despite continued adherence to universal, compulsory military service, they saw the rise of a more narrowly circumscribed standing army of personal followers that was to become the ruling class within the world empire. But despotism was a consequence of conquest, rather than the basis for the inauguration of a policy of conquest, the source of imperialist tendencies. Limitations on the royal power survived for a long time, as did the autonomy of the aristocracy, especially the ruling houses of the seven original tribes. This fact is readily understandable because the imperialist policy of the crown, instead of being at odds with the aristocracy, *rested on* it, merely formulated its policy. And the Persian people continued to occupy a position of preference within the empire. The king treated them with extreme care, offering them bounties and freedom from tribute. They constituted themselves the master class, though with a great measure of moderation. It was unnecessary to subject them to a special new system of military rule.

But the mere statement that we are here dealing with a "warrior nation" does not, of course, say everything. Indeed, this very character of the Persians as a warrior nation requires explanation. That explanation does not lie far afield. True, we do not know a great deal about the Persians before they entered into the limelight of history, but we do know enough about the prehistory of all Iranian Aryans to be able to reconstruct the prehistory of the Persians as well. It was geographic factors that made warriors of the Iranian Aryans. For them, war was the only method for keeping alive, the only possible form of life in a given environment. Warriors by environment, the Persians very probably reached the regions where history first finds them with sword in hand. And the psychological dispositions and organizational forms gained from such a mode of life persisted, continuing in an "objectless" manner. This is in accord with psychological developments that can be verified everywhere. The miser originally saves for good reasons, but beyond a certain point his hoarding ceases to be rational. The modern businessman acquires work habits because of the need for making a living, but labors far beyond the limits where acquisition still has rational meaning in the hedonist sense. Such phenomena have familiar parallels in the evolutionary facts of physical organisms and further parallels in the evolutionary facts of social phenomena, such as law, custom, and so on. Imperialism is such a phenomenon. The imperialism of a warrior nation, a people's imperialism, appears in history when a people has acquired a warlike disposition and a corresponding social organization *before* it has had an opportunity to be absorbed in the peaceful exploitation of its definitive area of settlement. Peoples who were so absorbed, such as the ancient Egyptians, the Chinese, or the Slavs, never of themselves develop imperialist tendencies, though they may be induced to do so by mercenary and generally alien armies. Peoples who were not preoccupied in this fashion—who were formed into a warlike pattern by their environment before they settled permanently, while they were still in a primitive stage of tribal or even clan organization —remain natural-born imperialists until centuries of peaceful work wear down that warlike disposition and undermine the corresponding social organization.

In the case of the Persians, we can thus understand what would otherwise remain incomprehensible—why the brief struggle for liberation from the Medes under Kurush II automatically turned into a war for the subjection of these former overlords and why this war reached out farther and farther. The Bactrians and Armenians were subjected. Babylon and Sardis were conquered. In the end Persian rule reached to the coast of Asia Minor, to the Caucasus and the Indus. A characteristic case was the conquest of Egypt by

Cambyses. The invasion was made as a matter of course. One side prepared for it, the other side anticipated it, just as though any other course were out of the question. And, as history testifies, the Hellenic world was utterly baffled as to the reasons for the campaign. Just as happens today, public opinion looked primarily to personal motives on the part of the ruling men—a line of inquiry that turns history into a form of gossip richly embroidered with romance. As for Cambyses, he was a warrior and the overlord of a mighty power. He needed deeds, for himself and for it. Egypt was not a particularly suitable object of aggression—but there it was, and so it was attacked. The truth of this interpretation is proved by the fact that the Persians never dreamed of stopping in Egypt but were intent on pushing on, to Siwah and Carthage on the one hand, and to the south on the other —even though there were no princesses to offer convenient pretexts for war. These further advances largely miscarried, and the difficulties in the way of further penetration proved to be insurmountable. But we have here a failure of military power rather than of the will to conquest. This was also true of the conquests of Darius I, who developed the despotic police state without bringing about a change in policy.

True, pretexts for war were always found. There is no situation in which such pretexts are altogether lacking. What matters here is that the pretexts are quite unsuitable to form links in the chain of explanation of historic events—unless history is to be resolved into an account of the whims of great lords. This, after all, is precisely the point at issue— why to some peoples any pretext was good enough for war, why to them war was the *prima* rather than the *ultima ratio,* the most natural activity in the world. This is the question of the nature of the imperialist mentality and constitutes our problem.

Even less satisfactory than the explanation by flimsy pre-texts is the theory that points to the interest in booty and tribute, or in commercial advantages. Of course such ele-ments are never lacking. Yet the Persians, of all conquerors were remarkably mild toward the peoples they subjugated

They never even remotely exploited them to the extent that would have been possible. Naturally they did seek some return from their conquests, once they had been made. The Persian king would become king of the country in question —as in the case of Egypt—or impose tribute or military levies on it. Yet there were never any cessions of privately owned land to Persians. The social organization of the conquered country usually remained intact. Religion, language, economic life suffered no harm. The leading men were often elevated to the imperial Persian aristocracy. Any concrete advantages were more in the nature of tokens of victory, esteemed as such, than of goals sought and exploited for their own sake.[1] Specifically nationalist trends are nowhere in evidence. The Persians did not "Persianize." In their proclamations, the kings often used several different languages. Unquestionably we have here a case of "pure" imperialism, unmixed with any element of nationalism. Any explanation derived from the cultural consequences which wars of conquest (at that time at least) could bring would be altogether inadmissible. Even today such cultural consequences are never consciously sought, in the sense that they could provide a decisive motive. Usually no one can foresee them clearly. There is no social force behind them. Moreover, they would be too much in the nature of "long-term promissory notes." In any event, they are beyond the mental horizon of the protagonists.

The religious element is conspicuously absent, with the Persians as with the Egyptians, a fact that is particularly noteworthy in the latter case. Both were tolerant to the point of indifference, especially the Persians, who actually fostered foreign cults. Outwardly this distinguishes their imperialism from that of the Assyrians. The Assyrians were Semites who migrated to Mesopotamia. They stuck to the upper reaches of the Tigris, where history finds them and whence they spread out, relatively undiluted by heterogeneous ethnic elements. Even Mesopotamia was not all—or nearly all—theirs until after the ninth century. Like the Persians, they were from the outset a "warrior nation," in the sense that has been defined; but, in contrast to the Persians, their organization, while aristocratic from earliest times, was along strictly despotic lines. The king himself was not divine, as in Egypt; he was merely the mandatory of the gods; yet despotism among the Assyrians was much more sharply marked than in Egypt, where it was regulated by a law higher than that of the king. Yet there is no evidence that a policy of imperialism was foisted on the Assyrian people by despotism. There was no special class of mercenaries, foreign or domestic. Down to the fall of Nineveh (606), massed native foot soldiers played an important role in the army. Battle chariots and cavalry were the weapons of the nobles, but they did not fight separately. War was the natural vocation of king and people. Culture, customs, script, religion, technology all came from Babylonia. The sovereigns who reigned in ancient Assur around 2000 called themselves Patísi, priest-kings. Not until about 1500, under Assur-bel-nishê-shu, did the royal title appear. This sacred character persisted in the Assyrian kingdom and in Assyrian policy. Assyrian wars were always, among other things, wars of religion, a fact that may be linked to their unmerciful cruelty. The enemy was always an "enemy of Assur."

At first Assyria expanded to the east and north, mostly at the expense of Babylonia. Once the borders of oldest Assyria, in the narrowest sense, had been crossed (under Assuruballit about 1400), there ensued a bloody struggle for command over the surrounding peoples and against Babylonia, a struggle that led to one success after another and, after a temporary setback in the thirteenth century, to a pinnacle under Tuklâtî-pal-ísharra I (1115-1100). Then came a time of quiescence for the peoples round about, but under Rammân-nirâri II (911-890) and especially Assurnasirpal (884-860) the policy of conquest that created the Assyrian world empire was inaugurated. Although interrupted by domestic strife and brief periods of exhaustion, it endured until the Scythian assault weakened it to such an extent that it succumbed quite suddenly to the Median-Babylonian coalition.

Year after year king and people took the field to conquer, lay waste, pillage, and murder, with pretext or without. The vanquished were crucified, impaled, flayed, immured alive by the thousands, or had their eyes put out or limbs struck off. Conquered cities were usually destroyed, the inhabitants often burned with them. Expressions like "grind into the dust" or "tinge the mountains with the blood of the foe" recur time and again in the annals of the kings. A relief sculpture from Khorsabad shows the king himself putting out the eyes of prisoners with a lance, holding the victim's head firm by means of a line fastened to a ring in his lower lip—an arrangement indicating that this was a routine procedure. It was not that the kings proceeded in this fashion only occasionally—say, in times of particular agitation. They all did it, without a single exception. The reason was, in part, that these wars were often intended as wars of annihilation. The enemy population was often resettled in the interior of the conquered country and replaced by Assyrians, and the survivors were subjected to a pitiless regime of exploitation. There was an effort at colonization and nationalization in order to weld into a single unit at least the regions that lay closest to old Assyria.

The first attacks were aimed at Babylonia—which defended itself longest—and at Armenia and Kurdistan. Then Syria and all the countries to the Phoenician shores of the Mediterranean were conquered, and finally portions of Asia Minor and even Egypt. Any hesitation to undertake a campaign seems to have been regarded as an extraordinary event. It *was*, in fact, exceptional, and when it occurred repeatedly, as under Assur-nirâri (755-746), it weakened the position of the crown. Yet not many complete successes were won. Babylonia was vanquished only at a late date (709 and 689), and then only temporarily. Other peoples were never subdued. Despite all the furious energy, the policy of violence failed time and again. Despite all the measures of annihilation, territory that had already been conquered had always to be conquered anew. The mistreated peoples defended themselves with savage desperation. Uprisings in the end passed over into wars of annihilation against the conqueror, and in 606 came the dramatic end.

What answer would we get if we were to ask an Assyrian king: "Why do you conquer without end? Why do you destroy one people after another, one city after another? Why do you put out the eyes of the vanquished? Why do you burn their habitations?" We would be told the official —perhaps even the conscious—motive. Tuklâtî-pal-ísharra I, for example, replied: "The God Assur, my Lord, commanded me to march. . . . I covered the lands of Saranit and Ammanit with ruins. . . . I chastized them, pursued their warriors like wild beasts, conquered their cities, took their gods with me. I made prisoners, seized their property, abandoned their cities to fire, laid them waste, destroyed them, made ruins and rubble of them, imposed on them the harshest yoke of my reign; and in their presence I made thank offerings to the God Assur, my Lord." Characteristically, this account reads much like Assurnasirpal's report of a hunt: "The gods Nindar and Nirgal, who cherish my priestly office, gave the beasts of the desert into my hands. Thirty mighty elephants I killed, 257 huge wild bulls I brought down with arrows from my open chariot, in the irresistible power of my glory."

Such an answer from the king does not help us much. It is scarcely permissible to assume that he was lying or pretending—nor would that matter, one way or the other. But we can scarcely be disputed when we insist that the God Assur commanded and his prophet—in this case the king himself—proclaimed merely what was in keeping with acquired habits of thought and the emotional response of the people, their "spirit," formed by their environment in the dim past. It is also plain that conscious motives—no matter whether, in the concrete case, they were always religious in character—are seldom *true* motives in the sense of being free of deceptive ideologies; and that they are never the *sole* motives. Human motivation is always infinitely complex, and we are never aware of all its elements. The Assyrian policy of conquest, like any similar policy, must have had many auxiliary motives. Lust for blood and booty, avarice and the craving for power, sexual impulses, commercial interests (more prominent with the Assyrians than the Persians)—all these, blended to varying degrees, may have played their part in motivating individuals and groups; also operative was the unrestrained will to gratify instincts—precisely those instincts to which a warlike past had given predominance in the mentality. Such real motives are powerful allies of official motives (whether religious or otherwise), increase their striking power, or usurp their guise. This aspect of imperialism emerges more sharply in the Assyrian case than in any other. But it is never altogether absent, not even today.

Here too, however, the actual foundation of the religious motive—and here is the crucial formulation—is the urge to action. The direction of this urge, determined by the nation's development, is, as it were, codified in religion. It is this, too, that makes the God Assur a war god and as such insatiable. For the fact of definite religious precepts can never be accepted as ultimate. It must always be explained. In the case of the Assyrians this is not at all difficult. That is why I placed the hunting account beside the war report. It is evident that the king and his associates regarded war and the chase from the same aspect of *sport*—if that expression is permissible. In their lives, war occupied the same role as sports and games do in present-day life. It served to gratify activity urges springing from capacities and inclinations that had once been crucial to survival, though they had now outlived their usefulness. Foreign peoples were the favorite game and toward them the hunter's zeal assumed the forms of bitter national hatred and religious fanaticism. War and conquest were not means but ends. They were brutal, stark naked imperialism, inscribing its character in the annals of history with the same fervor that made the Assyrians exaggerate the size of the muscles in their statuary.

Naturally, imperialism of this kind is worlds removed from the imperialism of later ages. Yet in its innermost nature the imperialism of Louis XIV, for example, ranks beside that of the Assyrians. True, it is more difficult to analyze. The "instinctual" element of bloody primitivism recedes, is softened and overgrown by the efforts of both actors and spectators to make these tendencies comprehensible to themselves and others, to found them on reason, to direct them toward reasonable aims—just as the popular mind seeks to rationalize ancient customs, legal forms, and dogmas, the living meaning of which has been lost. In an objective sense the results of such efforts are nearly always fallacious, but that does not mean that they lack all significance. They indicate functional changes in social habits, legal forms, and so on. They show how these modes of thought and behavior can either be adapted to a new social environment and made useful or be weakened by rationalist criticism. That is why the newer imperialisms no longer look like the Assyrian brand, and that is why they are more easily misunderstood. Only a more searching comparison will put them in their proper light. But we shall now add to the examples already cited—which were to introduce us to the nature and the problem of imperialism—certain others that will enable us to discuss individual points of interest and that will serve as a bridge to modern times.

In order to illuminate especially the character of the religious brand of imperialism, let us briefly discuss the case of the Arabs. The relevant facts are simple and uncontroverted. The Arabs were mounted nomads, a persistent warrior type, like the nomadic Mongol horsemen. At heart they have remained just that, despite all modifications of culture and organization. Only at a late date and incompletely did portions of the Arab people relinquish the equestrian profession —no one readjusts so slowly and with such difficulty as the mounted nomad. Such people are never able to support themselves alone, and in Arabia they constituted a master class that systematically exploited for its own purposes, sometimes by means of outright robbery, the (likewise Semitic) population that had settled here and there and was engaged in agriculture and trade. Internally the Arabs were organized along thoroughly democratic lines, again like all mounted nomads. It was a gentile and patriarchal type of democracy, in keeping with the "relations of production" that prevailed among a nation of herdsmen and horsemen, and quite different from agrarian and urban democracy—but democracy all the same in the sense that all members of the nation carried political weight and that all political expression grew from the people as a whole. The Arabs were divided into loosely knit tribes, headed by a freely elected sheik or emir who was dependent, in all affairs of importance, on the assent of the clan chiefs. The stock from which the tribes developed constituted the primary community, the fundamental social bond.

There were three elements that brought this Arab world to the stage of ferment. First of all, there was the alien rule of the Byzantines and Persians, of which, by the end of the sixth century, only Hejaz, Nejd, and Yemen had rid themselves. Secondly, in the realm of ideas, there was the religious bond that existed between the tribes. This was objectified in the ancient sanctuary of the Kaba at Mecca, where all the tribes met and were exposed to religious currents of every description, especially from the Semitic world, and where they created a cultural as well as a religious center. The center itself, the breeding place of new trends, was in the possession of a single tribe, the Koreishites, who thereby assumed a privileged position, often at odds with other interests. Even within the Koreish tribe the holy place was in charge of a special clique, as always happens in such cases. In the third place, an urban commercial culture, reaching out to draw in certain individuals, clans, and tribes, developed in the centers of communication, especially Mecca. This was bound to wear down many corners of the old order and way of life and thinking, at the same time opening a gulf between the elements so affected and the simple, old-style Bedouins, to whom these things appeared alien and dissonant. There appeared, at first purely by way of reaction, a movement of social reform or revolution, beginning in the early seventh century. Pristine simplicity, a softening of the contrasts between poor and rich, a voluntary relinquishment of the pursuit of profit—these were Mohammed's first thoughts. He threw down the gage of battle to established interest and "acquired right," and his first practical demand was for a purge of the stain of money-grubbing by means of alms-giving.

Whatever his adherents may have thought, the interests that were threatened recognized the situation with the clarity peculiar to them and acted promptly. But their measures failed to destroy Mohammed, merely driving him out, and only a year after the Hegira he was able to make himself master of Medina. Thus all they succeeded in doing was to force him, first, onto the defensive and, then, the offensive, with a corresponding shift in his viewpoint. The reformer of the sacred tribe became the aggressive fighter against the "Infidels." Inner communion gave way to the call for war on behalf of the faith—the jihad—as the most important practical demand, the normal outward attitude of the faithful. Partly as a cause of this ideological orientation, partly as its consequence, there came into being a practical fighting organization, which reduced the element of inner communion to the role of a means for self-discipline on the part of the warrior, and to which the Bedouins took like ducks to water. Both ideology and organization proved their vitality and grew with the task for which they had been created—the struggle for Mecca and the unifying conversion of the Arab tribes. And when, suddenly, they had arrived, become firm, grown into a power, they followed the impulse they had received. Mohammed himself attempted to reach beyond Arabia (the campaign of Said), though without success. Abu Bekr, having developed the new politico-military organization and secured it against uprisings, invaded Syria without difficulty. Yet the new clerical warrior state remained democratic, despite the Caliph's wealth of temporal and clerical power. It could do so, because it had grown straight from the people. Loot was community property, to be distributed according to military rank. Not until Othman was the acquisition of land in the conquered countries permitted. The original idea had been that the Arabs would remain a master class, merely establishing garrisons. Under Omar, Persia was invaded—without any good reason, but with brilliant success. Byzantine Syria suffered the same fate at almost the same time. Then came Palestine, Phoenicia, Egypt. Christians and Jews were expelled from Arabia, forbidden to use Arab script and language. After a period of confusion came the culmination, under the Omayyads (661-750), when the center of empire shifted to Damascus. Ideology and organization began to lose their original impact. There was increasing differentiation and division of labor. The Arabs began to fuse with the conquered countries, and developing despotism did its work. Rigid centralism succumbed and the Occidental Caliphate separated from the Oriental. The Arab wave spent itself against Byzantium. But the basic outlines remained. North Africa and Spain were conquered. Frankish might rather than any lack of Arab will put an end to further penetration. In Asia it was the same story. Many armed actions still succeeded. A halt was called only when it was impossible to push on. And whenever a halt was called, internal difficulties erupted, destroying the empire in the end.

The diagnosis is simple. We are here face to face with a "warrior nation" and must explain from its circumstances how it came to be one. We see how internal struggles gave rise to a unified war organization behind which rallied all the popular forces—including those in the ideological sphere —a war machine that, once in motion, continued so long as there was steam behind it and it did not run up against a stone wall.[2] War was the normal function of this military theocracy. The leaders might discuss methods, but the basic issue was never in question. This point emerges with particular clarity, since the Arabs, for the most part, never troubled to look for even flimsy pretexts for war, nor did they even declare war. Their social organization needed war; without successful wars it would have collapsed. War, moreover, was the normal occupation of the members of the society. When there was no war, they would rebel or fall upon each other over theological controversies. The older social doctrine, especially the tendency to guard against merging with the conquered land and to keep the people fixed in the profession of arms, served the needs of this situation. Whenever that failed, whenever a new environment beckoned in another country with a richer background, whenever the Arabs settled down there, especially when they acquired land—then the impetus of war was spent and there developed such cultural centers as Cordoba, Cairo, and Bagdad. The energies of the best elements were diverted to other goals. We have, then, a typical case of "objectless," violent expansion, born of past necessities of life, grown to the proportions of a powerful drive by virtue of long habit, persisting to the point of exhaustion—a case of imperialism which we are able to view historically, precisely, and completely from its very origins to its death in the functional transformation of its energy.

What was the role played by the religious element, the commandments of Allah, the doctrine of the Prophet? These pervaded and dominated Arab life with an intensity that has few parallels in history. They determined daily conduct, shaped the whole world outlook. They permeated the mentality of the believer, made him someone who was characteristically different from all other men, opened up an unbridgeable gulf between him and the infidel, turning the latter into the arch enemy with whom there could be no true peace. These influences can be traced into every last detail of Arab policy. And most conspicuous of all in the whole structure of precepts is the call to holy war that opens wide the gates of paradise.

Yet if one sought to conclude that the religious element played a causative role in the Arab policy of conquest, that imperialism rooted in religion must therefore be a special phenomenon, one would come up against three facts. In the first place, it is possible to comprehend Arab policy quite apart from the religious element. It rises from factors that would have been present even without Allah's commandments and presumably would have taken effect even without them—as we saw in the example of the Persians. Some aspects of Arab imperialism may make sense only in the light of the Word of the Prophet, but its basic force we must clearly place elsewhere. In the second place, it was by no means true that religion was an independent factor that merely happened to be tending in the same direction as the imperialist drive for conquest. The interrelation between the Word of the Prophet and the data of the social environment (that by themselves already explain that drive) is too obvious to be overlooked. It was the Prophet of the mounted no-mads who proclaimed war everlasting—not just *any* prophet. We simply cannot ignore the fact that such preachments came naturally to the Prophet and his followers. We cannot dispose of the question by positing a theoretical dominance and creative social force somehow peculiar to the religious element—as though some mysterious and unfathomable vi-sion, remote from environmental pressures, had given rise to the Word of the Prophet in a vacuum, as it were, and as though that Word alone had driven the people forward *in agmen, in pulverem, in clamorem.* It is pointless to insist that the Word of the Prophet is an ultimate fact beyond which social science analysis cannot go, any more than it can transcend the data of physical nature—when that fact becomes easily understandable from the very social, psychic, and physical background that is itself quite adequate to ex-plain fully what the Word of the Prophet is otherwise left to explain alone. Quite apart from trying to explain the unknown through the still less known, we would be resort-ing to a crutch that is quite unnecessary. But suppose we do accept the theory that the Prophet's doctrine existed *in vacuo.* In trying to understand its success, we would—to mention the third point—inevitably come up against the same situation that confronted us when we sought to grasp its basic spirit. It is only necessary to visualize what might have happened if the jihad had been preached to the un-military "fishermen" of Galilee, the "little people" in Pales-tine. Is it really far-fetched to assume that they would not have followed the call, that they *could* not have followed it, that, had they tried any such thing, they would have failed wretchedly and destroyed their own community? And if, conversely, Mohammed had preached humility and submission to his Bedouin horsemen, would they not have turned their backs on him? And if they *had* followed him, would not *their* community have perished? A prophet does more than merely formulate a message acceptable to his early adherents; he is successful and comprehensible only when he also formulates a policy that is *valid* at the moment. This is precisely what distinguishes the successful—the "true"— prophet from his unsuccessful fellow—the "false" prophet. The "true" prophet recognizes the necessities of the existing situation—a situation that exists quite independently of him—and when these necessities subsequently change, he manages to adopt a new policy without letting the faithful feel that this transition is treachery.

I do not think this view can be disputed. What it means is that even in this highly charismatic case no causative role can be ascribed to the Word of the Prophet and that Arab imperialism must not be looked on as something unrelated to other imperialisms. What is true of Arab imperialism is true of any imperialism bearing a religious "coloration"— as we may now put it. This applies to states and peoples, but not, of course, to the expansive drives of religious communities as such—that of the Catholic Church in the Middle Ages, for example. It too did not shrink from brute force and resort to religious warfare. Too often it exploited the instinct for conquest—which played an important part in the Crusades, for example—and often served the instinct for power as well—as in the case of many a Pope. Whenever it was dominated by a state, as happened at times, for example under the Roman emperors and later under Charlemagne and Henry III, the expansive drive of the faith at once showed signs of merging into the expansive trend of the state in question; and if this did not happen on a more intensive scale, it was only because the relationship between the universal state and the Church never endured for very long. Such incidents, however, remained accessory aberrations; for, by and large and to an ever-increasing degree, the Church maintained itself as a specifically clerical, super-governmental, and supernational power, not merely ideologically but also practically, in accordance with the power resources and organizational methods at its disposal. Hence its will to conquest remained a mere will to convert. In the course of this mission of conversion and in the political interests of the Church, the military subjugation of one country by another might on occasion be desirable, but it was never an end in itself. Conversion without such conquest would have been—and usually was—sufficient in such cases. The ideologically appropriate method—and the customary one—was the sermon. What needed to be spread was the rule of dogma and the corresponding organization of religious, not political, life. In this process natural instincts of pugnacity could be vented only incidentally and rarely. This is clearly seen from the characteristic fact that the devoutly Catholic Spaniards never dreamed of giving a religious motivation to their overseas conquests, though these conquests did indeed serve the interests of the Church.[3] Here, then, there is an essentially different element that would stamp such a religious imperialism as something distinct, something with outright religious causation—if, that is, we can really speak of imperialism in this case. We do not propose to do so and are holding this phenomenon up to view only to the extent that it interacts with the imperialisms of nations and states.

The Arabs, for their part, did not proselytize. When the inhabitants of conquered countries adopted Mohammedanism *en masse,* this was not the result of a deliberate plan by the conquerors, though it was an entirely plausible process of adaptation. Nor did the Arabs annihilate the infidels. On the contrary, they were treated with remarkable mildness. Neither conversion nor annihilation would have accorded with the Arab brand of war on behalf of the faith. From the viewpoint of their interests, neither course would have paid, for they were dependent on the labor and tribute of subjugated peoples for their livelihood, for their chance to remain a parasitical warrior and master nation. Once the infidel was converted or killed, an object of exploitation was lost, an element that was necessary to Arab life, and social organization was sacrificed. Thus the Arabs were quite content to leave the infidels their faith, their lives, and their property. Let them remain infidels. What mattered was that they must serve the faithful. There was never any objection that such a policy might be wrong since it perpetuated the existence of infidels—an argument that should carry much weight with religious sentiment and that was, indeed, always decisive in the case of Christian sentiment as embodied in the Catholic Church. However this policy may fit into the inner logic of the Mohammedan religion,[4] it *was* Arab practice. And this is precisely what characterizes the position of the religious element in this case. The meaning of the struggle was not the spreading of the faith but the spreading of Arab rule—in other words, war and conquest for their own sake.

This does not, of course, mean that we deny the significance of religious commandments in the consciousness of the people. Had an Arab been asked why he fought, he might, as a born warrior, on proper reflection have countered with the question as to why one lived. That is how self-evident, how far above all rational thought, war and the urge for expansion were to him. But he would not have given such a reply. He would have said: "I fight because Allah and his Prophet will it." And this reply gave him an emotional prop in his struggle, provided him with a mode of conduct that preserved his character as a warrior. Religion was more than a mere reflex, certainly within the body social. It is not my intention to pursue this approach to the extreme, particularly since we here touch on problems that reach far too deeply to be disposed of within the framework of our topic. It was for that reason that I emphasized just now the possibility of the religious idea's taking on a social life of its own, in the example of Christianity. But the imperialism of a people or a state can never be explained in this fashion.

Arab imperialism was, among other things, a form of

popular imperialism. In examining this type at greater length, let us select the example of the ancient Germans. We know far too little of their prehistory to be able to assert that they were a warrior nation in our sense during that period. It is probable that they were not—this is indicated by the high stage of development that agriculture had attained among them—which does not rule out that certain tribes, at an early date, acquired warlike habits by piracy, enslavement, and so on. True, the picture of them drawn by Tacitus does not accord with the assumption that the Germans were an agricultural people, with an aristocracy that was neither large nor exalted. Other reports likewise fail to support such a view, which, nevertheless, prevailed rather uniformly among historians down to the year 1896. Wittich, Knapp, and Hildebrand then raised their voices in opposition, though it does not seem that their views will prevail. In any event, the Great Migrations made warrior nations of the Germanic tribes (similar circumstances had had this result even earlier in the case of the Cimbrians and Teutons)—especially those tribes that had to traverse great distances. Even these, however, usually lacked the imperialist *élan*. They were looking for new areas of settlement, nothing more. When they found such areas, they were content. They did not reach farther and farther—they were too weak for that. It is true that the East and West Goths, the Vandals, and the Lombards did constitute themselves as military master peoples, but that was a necessity from the point of view of self-preservation. We find only one indubitable case of imperialism—that of the Salian Franks. Since the third century, alliances had welded together their various tribes and in the fourth and fifth centuries they spread westward across the Rhine, following the retreating Roman legions. All the while they clung to their tribal territory, but on the other hand they displaced or destroyed the Roman-Celtic population, actually and continually expanding their national domain. This paved the way for the far-reaching policies of Clovis I, who first began vigorous attacks on the Roman power (Battle of Soissons, 486) and shifted the center of his empire to Paris, then exterminated his Frankish co-princes, thereby uniting all Franks, and finally subjugated even Germanic tribes (first the Alemanni, then the Burgundians, and at last the West Goths in Aquitania). Despite the division of the empire, Clovis' successors continued his policies, at first with some success (subjugation of Thuringia, completion of the conquest of Burgundy, adherence of Bavaria). This policy of conquest was typical imperialism. Without any regard for "interests" or "pretexts"—though the latter, of course, were always at hand—indeed, sometimes without the slightest pretext at all, Clovis and his immediate successors simply reached out as far as their power permitted—into limitless space, as it were. There was not even a major organizational principle, as is shown by the division of the empire. The Franks were simply driven forward by instincts of war and power. The report by Gregory of Tours reads like a report about the Assyrian kings. The religious element played precisely the same role. Gregory has his hero say, before the attack on Aquitania: "I am furious that these Arians rule any part of Gaul. With God's help we shall take the field and subject the land to our will." The account of the murders of the other Frankish princes closes with these words: "Thus, day after day, God felled the enemies of Clovis the Christian under His fist, for Clovis walked in the path of righteousness and his deeds were pleasing in the eyes of the Lord."

This was a popular imperialism. True, the royal power grew with its successes, with the direct acquisition of vast areas of land—quite apart from the controversial question of its "sovereignty" over all land—with control over the Church, and, finally with the allegiance of an ever-growing number of warriors and other beneficiaries of war who were directly dependent on the crown. Yet the whole people still participated—insofar as they carried political weight. This meant not merely the uppermost stratum—although even then the organization of society was rather aristocratic in character—nor did it mean a special warrior class. The kings still depended on the approval of broad groups much more than on the "powerful." Their own power was neither so unlimited nor so firm that they could afford to pursue unpopular policies. There may be much room for controversy about the social structure of the Merovingian period, but the conclusion is inescapable that the imperialist will to battle and conquest was the people's will, and that the king could have been no more than the leader and spokesman of this wide-spread disposition.

This is entirely plausible. Struggles for the maintenance and extension of their area of settlement had temporarily made a warrior nation of the Franks. In this fashion alone can an entire people become oriented toward imperialism, and that is what happened to the Franks. Our example enables us to observe not only the origin but also the gradual disappearance of imperialist tendencies. In the case of the Franks, the "habit of conquest" did not go back far enough to become enduringly fixed, as in the case of the Arabs. Even while they were engaged in conquest, the Franks remained predominantly tillers of the soil. Unlike the Arabs, they did not constitute themselves an armed camp in enemy territory. Thus the popular will to conquest as such soon vanished, once large numbers of Franks had ensconced themselves comfortably in new areas of settlement—the upper strata, in part, also among alien populations of the empire. Once again they were swallowed up by the private sphere of agriculture, hunting, local guerrilla warfare—the life of village, estate, and province. The people very soon lost all interest in imperial politics, all contact with the central power. They insisted vigorously on protecting themselves against excessive central authority at home and adventure abroad. This explains why the empire was always on the verge of flying apart, why the temporal and clerical powers so readily obtained the "Magna Carta" of 614, why after the middle of the seventh century local authorities arose everywhere. Despite the prospect of booty and the opportunities which war then opened up to individuals, the masses began to resent universal military service, the nobles their feudal service. True, the Franks did remain a belligerent people.

They eagerly resorted to arms. But they could no longer be enlisted on behalf of plans of unlimited conquest, for a policy that would remove them from their homes and interests too often for long periods of time. We see that not every warlike nation tends toward imperialism. There must be other circumstances, especially forms of social organization. Above all, in order to exhibit a continual trend toward imperialism, a people must not live on—or at least not be absorbed by— its own labor. When that happens, the instincts of conquest are completely submerged in the economic concerns of the day. In such a case even the nobles—unless a special military class arises—cannot evade the economic pressure, even though they themselves may remain parasitical in an economic sense. They become content with the peaceful administration of their estates and offices, with hunting and local skirmishing.

In this connection it is interesting to compare the second, Carolingian wave of Frankish imperialism with the Merovingian wave that preceded it. If Merovingian imperialism was definitely "popular" in character, Carolingian just as certainly was not. Even the older Carolingians, who reunited the empire before Charlemagne, had to resort to special measures to muster an army against the Arabs. They were compelled to organize a special warrior class with an economic base of its own, professional knights, subsisting on Church lands. The people failed to support the crown, except in the case of an undertaking in the immediate vicinity of their homes, and the crown thus had to create a special group of vassals. These had to be enabled to live without working, if they were to be readily available—in other words, they needed benefices. Thus the feudal system arose, the technical innovation of the mounted army being far more a consequence than a cause of this social development. True, Charlemagne still resorted to the general levy, but in the face of rising resistance, as seen from the importance popularly attributed to draft indemnities. The people fled from the imperialism of the crown into protective dependence on local authority. And it was the vassals who were the

main support of Charlemagne's imperialist policies, even in
a political sense. This emerged quite characteristically early
in his reign, in his differences with Carloman. It was precisely imperialism that was at stake in this controversy.
Carloman sought peace with the Lombards, and he was
supported by the people who "counted." Charlemagne
wanted war with them, as a first step along his path of a
universal imperialism embroidered with Roman and religious elements. Charlemagne and his policies prevailed.
But his successors failed because their peoples, though aris-
tocratically organized, were basically anti-imperialist.

Let us add that these observations also apply to the imperialism, centering in Italy, of the German kings of the Middle Ages. Historians are fond of speculating what may have
persuaded Otto I to undertake his Italian campaign, for they
rightly find his motives obscure. Such inquiry into personal
motivation is futile and irrelevant. All the German kings who
pursued such a policy faced the same situation. Their power
rested primarily on the political and economic position
of their dynasties, which was independent of the royal title.
As the chiefs of their tribes they had estates, vassals, legiti-
mate usufructs within their territory, and the opportunity to
exploit their people even beyond legal limits. Acquisition of
the crown gained them imperial estates and usufructs, sovereignty over the independent cities, and intimate contact with
high ecclesiastics and imperial vassals. Actually, however,
their fellow dukes and princes could be counted among these
royal vassals to only a limited degree. Instead, they felt themselves to be relatively independent powers in their own right.
Each king had to win their allegiance anew, sometimes actually to subdue them. They were unwilling either to let the
king interfere in the internal affairs of their territories, or to
give unconditional support to any foreign policy. These territories, after all, were not mere administrative districts, but
living political entities with interests of their own. For every
one of the Ottonians, Salians, and Hohenstaufens, the conquest of power within the empire was the primary task.
When that had been solved to some degree, each of them

had a fighting organization of his own, a feudal army enlisted under his banner which needed work and subsistence.
At the same time each of them knew how narrow was the
foundation on which he stood, how quickly success, once
gained, might be frittered away. Above all, in order to rule
Germany they needed money, for the amount of land that
could be handed out was limited and, besides, every enfeoffment soon alienated the liegeman from the crown. Germany
was unable to offer such funds to the crown, not because of
poverty, but because of its form of organization. The kings
therefore needed a territory where they might rule absolutely, not merely as feudal overlords. Italy was such a territory. Its conquest would preoccupy the feudal army—satisfy it, tie it firmly to the king, weld it into a professional
army. Had it really been possible to conquer Italy, all the
German elements that were avid for war and booty would
have rallied to the royal colors. The king would have been
able to pay them and perhaps to conquer the entire Mediterranean basin. This would have automatically made him master of Germany as well, for the local centers of authority
would have lost their warriors to him—would have become
deflated, as it were. Whatever may have been in the mind of
Otto I, this was the situation and this was the meaning of
the Italian policy. We see it most clearly in Frederick II, who
quite probably pursued it in full awareness of the goal of
ruling Italy by the power of German knighthood, and ruling
Germany by the power of Italian money, making both countries his base for a far-reaching policy of conquest. Thus a
policy otherwise suggesting an almost incredible lack of political sagacity becomes entirely comprehensible. It was quite
safe to dole out the remaining imperial and dynastic lands in
Germany, to surrender one royal prerogative after another
to the princes, to sacrifice even the cities responsible directly
to the crown—in other words, to deprive the royal power in
Germany of its basis—for the sake of a temporary respite.
All this was quite safe—*if* there was the hope of creating in
Italy, far more effectively than by guerrilla warfare with the
German princes, a mighty bastion of power that would

serve to regain the relinquished positions in Germany. Frederick II came close to attaining this goal. He created the state of Naples for himself and was able to function as its despot. Had he met with success against the Pope and the Lombards, he would have become master of the situation even in Germany; and undoubtedly enterprises in the nature of crusades—such as Frederick II actually inaugurated— would have followed, as would have, perhaps, attacks on France and Spain. But full success was wanting, and the whole policy ended in disaster for the imperial power. The essential meaning of the policy had been to strengthen the royal power even in Germany, but when only its negative rather than its positive fruits were realized, it appeared as a policy of surrender to regional authority, the pointless pursuit of a phantom. In essence the policy was imperialist. But it was the imperialism of a ruler rather than of a people. That is precisely why it failed, for the people and the nobles would have none of it. And because it failed, the royal power bled to death. Here we have an interesting example of an anti-imperialist warrior aristocracy.

Within the framework of the present study, we can be concerned only with examining our problem with the help of certain typical examples; yet we shall briefly glance at two further instances where the diagnosis is subject to certain doubts. The first case is the imperialism of Alexander the Great. The essential feature is that here, instead of the founding of a new world empire by piling conquest on conquest—which takes much time, a sharply focused will on the part of the ruling classes of a people, or a long succession of despots—instead of this, the central power of an already existing empire was overturned by a swift blow, only to be picked up by the victor. It would not have been very much different if some Persian satrap had led a successful rebellion and lifted himself into the saddle. That this was so is clearly seen from the fact that Alexander, once he had reached his goal, at once established himself as a Persian king. While he was intent on rewarding his Macedonians and preserving their military power, he could not even dream of making them a ruling people. True, he penetrated beyond the frontiers of the Persian empire, but this was nothing but an essentially individual adventure. He availed himself of the Macedonian military machine, which had grown to maturity, first in the struggle for the coast of Macedonia itself, and then in a miniature imperialism against the Scythians and Greeks, and which was on the verge of attacking Persia even without him; yet he transformed the situation into a policy that was anything but Macedonian imperialism. Nor was there anything that one might be tempted to call Greek cultural imperialism. Obviously the domain of Greek culture expanded by virtue of Alexander's conquests, but not substantially more than it would have done in the course of time even without him. What was aggressive in this situation was neither Greek culture, nor Greek commercial interest, but a warrior who saw the tempting bait of a great empire before him. This was neither the imperialism of a state, nor that of a people, but rather a kind of individual imperialism that is of no further interest to us, akin to but not identical with the imperialism of the Caesars, that is to say, of politicians whose stature rises with their military missions, who need ever new military successes to maintain their position—men like Julius Caesar himself and Napoleon I, for example.

The second case on which we shall touch is the imperialism of Rome. We must bear in mind above all in this connection that the policy of the Empire was directed only toward its preservation and therefore was not imperialist within our definition. True, there was almost continuous warfare, because the existing situation could be maintained only by military means. Individual emperors (Germanicus, for example) might wage war for its own sake, in keeping with our definition, but neither the Senate nor the emperors were generally inclined toward new conquests. Even Augustus did no more than secure the frontiers. After Germanicus had been recalled, Tiberius tried to put into effect a policy of peace toward the Germans. And even Trajan's conquests can be explained from a desire to render the empire more tenable. Most of the emperors tried to solve the problem by concessions and appeasement. But from the Punic Wars to Augustus there was undoubtedly an imperialist period, a time of unbounded will to conquest.

The policies of this epoch are not as naively manifest as those in the other cases discussed so far. Here is the classic example of that kind of insincerity in both foreign and domestic affairs which permeates not only avowed motives but also probably the conscious motives of the actors themselves —of that policy which pretends to aspire to peace but unerringly generates war, the policy of continual preparation for war, the policy of meddlesome interventionism. There was no corner of the known world where some interest was not alleged to be in danger or under actual attack. If the interests were not Roman, they were those of Rome's allies; and if Rome had no allies, then allies would be invented. When it was utterly impossible to contrive such an interest—why, then it was the national honor that had been insulted. The fight was always invested with an aura of legality. Rome was always being attacked by evil-minded neighbors, always fighting for a breathing space. The whole world was pervaded by a host of enemies, and it was manifestly Rome's duty to guard against their indubitably aggressive designs. They were enemies who only waited to fall on the Roman people. Even less than in the cases that have already been discussed, can an attempt be made here to comprehend these wars of conquest from the point of view of concrete objectives. Here there was neither a warrior nation in our sense, nor, in the beginning, a military despotism or an aristocracy of specifically military orientation. Thus there is but one way to an understanding: scrutiny of domestic class interests, the question of who stood to gain.

It was certainly not the Italian peasant. The conquests gained him nothing—on the contrary, they made possible competition on the part of foreign grain, one of the causes for his disappearance. He may not have been able to foresee that eventuality in the republican period, but he did feel all the more keenly the burden of military service that was always interfering with his concerns, often destroying his livelihood. True, it was this class that gave rise to the caste of professional soldiers who remained in the military service beyond the minimum term of enlistment. But in the first place, the rise of that estate was only a consequence of the policy of war, and, in the second place, even these people had no real interest in war. They were not impelled by savage pugnacity, but by hope for a secure old age, preferably the allotment of a small farm. And the veteran would much rather have such a farm at home than somewhere in Syria or Britain. As for war booty, the emperor used it to pay his debts or to stage circuses at Rome. The soldiers never saw much of it. The situation of the Roman proletariat was different. Owing to its peculiar position as the democratic puppet of ambitious politicians and as the mouthpiece of a popular will inspired by the rulers, it did indeed get the benefit of much of the booty. So long as there was good reason to maintain the fiction that the population of Rome constituted the Roman people and could decide the destinies of the empire, much did depend on its good temper, and mass corruption was the stock-in-trade of every political career. But again, the very existence, in such large numbers, of this proletariat, as well as its political importance, was the consequence of a social process that also explains the policy of conquest. For this was the causal connection: the occupation of public land and the robbery of peasant land formed the basis of a system of large estates, operating extensively and with slave labor. At the same time the displaced peasants streamed into the city and the soldiers remained landless—hence the war policy.

The latifundian landowners were, of course, deeply interested in waging war. Quite apart from the fact that they needed slaves, whom war provided in the cheapest way, their social and economic position—that of the senatorial aristocracy—would have become untenable the moment the Roman citizen thought he was menaced by an enemy and might have to fight for the interests or the honor of the country. The alternative to war was agrarian reform. The landed aristocracy could counter the perpetual threat of revolution only with the glory of victorious leadership. Had it remained an aristocracy of large yeomen or become one of landed nobles—as was the aristocracy of the German Middle Ages and of the later empire—its position would not have been so dangerous. But it was an aristocracy of landlords, large-scale agricultural entrepreneurs, born of struggle against their own people. It rested solely on control of the state machine. Its only safeguard lay in national glory. Its only possible course was preoccupation with the foreign-policy contingencies of the state, which were in any case a mystery to the citizens.

This does not mean that the individual senator, when he pleaded for another war, was always mindful of these circumstances. Such things never rise into full consciousness. An unstable social structure of this kind merely creates a general disposition to watch for pretexts for war—often held to be adequate with entire good faith—and to turn to questions of foreign policy whenever the discussion of social problems grew too troublesome for comfort. The ruling class was always inclined to declare that the country was in danger, when it was really only class interests that were threatened. Added to this, of course, were groups of every description who were interested in war, beginning with the political type we have called the Caesar—a type that often went farther than the Senate liked, creating situations where it sometimes became necessary to apply the brakes—and reaching down to army suppliers and those leeches in the conquered provinces, the procurators who represented the conquering military leaders. But here too we deal with consequences rather than causes. And another consequence that always emerges in imperialism was the phenomenon that the policy of conquest inevitably led to situations that compelled further conquests. Once this road was entered upon, it was difficult to call a halt, and finally the results far transcended what anyone had originally desired or aspired to. Indeed, such a policy almost automatically turned against the very aims for the sake of which it had been designed. The empire became ungovernable, even by an aristocracy as highly gifted in a political sense as was the Roman. It evaded the rule of that aristocracy, and in the end military despotism went over the heads of the aristocrats and passed on to the order of the day. History offers no better example of imperialism rooted in the domestic political situation and derived from class structure.

IMPERIALISM IN THE MODERN ABSOLUTE MONARCHY

At the threshold of modern Europe there stands a form of imperialism that is of special interest to us. It is rooted in the nature of the absolutist state of the seventeenth and eighteenth centuries which was, everywhere on the Continent, the result of the victory of the monarchy over the estates and classes. Everywhere on the Continent, in the sixteenth and seventeenth centuries, these struggles broke the political back of the people, leaving only the prince and his soldiers and officials on the devastated soil of earlier political factions. Of the whole family of constitutions in western and central Europe, only the English constitution maintained itself. Whenever there was enough power and activity in the autocratic state, imperialist tendencies began to stir, notably in Spain, France, and the larger territories of Germany. Let us take France as an example.

Of the eight virtually independent principalities that threatened to divide the West Frankish empire among themselves on the decline of the Carolingians, the duchy of France, through the rise of the Capets, came to be the foundation not only of the royal title but also of a royal policy that, despite certain relapses, continued steadfastly. Even Abbé Suger, under Louis VI and Louis VII, had already formulated the principles that were ultimately to lead that policy to victory. The obvious aims were to fight against the other seven principalities and against the rural nobility, which in France, too, enjoyed virtual independence and lived only for its private feuds and its own undertakings abroad. The obvious tactics were the representation of the interests of the Church, the cities, and the peasantry, with the help of a small standing army (*maison du roi*, originally formed from a few hundred poor noblemen). The Hundred Years' War with England served to develop national sentiment and to bring the kingship to the fore. It had the effect of rallying the immense war potential of the aristocracy to the crown and of gradually disciplining the aristocracy as well. Crusades and other foreign operations were contributory factors. As early as Saint Louis, the kingship rested on a broad political foundation which was quite equal to the revolts of the nobles that kept breaking out all the time, and also to the power of the Popes. As early as the last Capet an orderly tax administration had developed. The house of Valois continued the policy—more accurately, the policy continued under that dynasty, for nothing is further from our mind than to seek to explain a historical process simply by the actions of individuals. Charles V temporarily subdued the nobility and mastered the cities for good, subjecting them to a policy of mercantilism. Under Charles VII the army was reorganized along modern lines (1439) and a larger standing army was established. Louis XI completed the construction of the unified national state, and under him the provincial estates lost much of their importance. The internecine warfare among the nobles during the religious wars of the sixteenth century did the rest, and from there the road led, by way of Sully and Richelieu, to the culmination of this development in Louis XIV. Let us examine his situation.

He was master of the machinery of state. His ancestors had gradually created this position by military force; or rather, in a military sense, it had been created in the course of the development of the national state, for that course manifested itself in military struggle, and the centralized state could arise only when one of the military powers originally present triumphed over the others, absorbing what was left of them in the way of military strength and initiative. In France, as elsewhere, the absolutist national state meant the military organization of the martial elements of the nation, in effect a war machine. True, this was not its entire meaning and cultural significance. Now that national unity was achieved, now that, since the victory over Spain, no external enemy offered a serious threat any longer, there might have been disarmament—the military element might have been permitted to recede. The state would not have ceased to exist or failed to fulfill its function on that account. But the foundations of royal power rested on this military character of the state and on the social factors and psychological tendencies it expressed. Hence it *was* maintained, even though the causes that had brought it to the fore had disappeared. Hence the war machine continued to impress its mark on the state. Hence the king felt himself to be primarily a warlord, adorned himself preeminently with military emblems. Hence his chief concern was to maintain a large, well-equipped army, one that remained active and was directly tied to his person. All other functions he might delegate to his subordinates. But this one—supreme command of the army and with it the direction of foreign affairs—he claimed as his own prerogative. When he was unable to exercise it, he at least made a pretense of personal military efficiency. Any other inadequacy he and the dominant groups might have pardoned. Military shortcomings, however, were dangerous, and when they were present—which doubtless was the case with Louis XIV—they had to be carefully concealed. The king might not actually be a hero in battle, but he had to have the reputation of being one.

The necessity for this attitude flows from the social structure of the period. In a political sense neither the peasantry nor the working masses carried weight—and this was true in the social sense as well. In its fight against the nobility, the crown had occasionally championed both, but essentially they were and remained helots, to be disposed of at will—

not only economically exploited but even, against their will, trained to be blindly obeying soldiers. The urban middle class was also virtually beholden to the crown, though not quite so unconditionally. Once a valuable ally in the struggle against the nobility, it had become a mere servant. It had to obey, was molded by the crown along the lines of greatest financial return. The Church likewise paid for its national opposition to Rome with strict submission to the royal power. To this extent the king was actually, not merely legally, the master. It was of little concern to him—within eventually quite wide limits—what all these people who were forced to submit to him thought. But that was not true of the aristocracy. It too had had to submit to the crown, surrendering its independence and political rights—or at least the opportunity to exercise them. The stiff-necked rural nobility that once had both feet firmly planted in the soil amid its people had turned into a court aristocracy of extreme outward servility. Yet its social position remained intact. It still had its estates, and its members had retained their prestige in their own immediate neighborhoods. The peasants were more or less at its mercy. Each of the great houses still had its dependent circle among the lower nobility. Thus the aristocracy as a whole was still a power factor that had to be taken into account. Its submission to the crown was more in the nature of a settlement than a surrender. It resembled an election—a compulsory one, to be sure—of the king as the leader and executive organ of the nobility. Politically the nobility ruled far more completely *through* the king than it once did while it challenged his power. At that time, after all, the still independent cities did form a modest counterpoise to the nobility. Had the king, for example, conceived the notion of translating into action his pose as the protector of the lowest population strata, the nobility woud have been able to squelch any such attempt by mere passive resistance—as happened in Austria in the case of Joseph II. The nobles would have merely had to retire to their châteaux in order to bring into play, even outwardly, the actual foundations of their power, in order to become again a reasonably independent rural nobility which would have been capable of putting up a good fight.

The reason they did no such thing was, in essence, because the king did what they wanted and placed the domestic resources of the state at their disposal. But the king was aware of the danger. He was carefully intent on remaining the leader of the aristocracy. Hence he drew its members to his court, rewarded those that came, sought to injure and discredit those that did not. He endeavored successfully to have only those play a part who had entered into relations with him and to foster the view, within the aristocracy, that only the *gens de la cour*—court society—could be considered to have full and authoritative standing. Viewed in this light, those aspects that historians customarily dispose of as court extravagance and arbitrary and avoidable mismanagement take on an altogether different meaning. It was a class rather than an individual that was actually master of the state. That class needed a brilliant center, and the court had to be such a center—otherwise it might all too readily have become a parliament. But whoever remained away from his estates for long periods of time was likely to suffer economic loss. The court had to indemnify him if it wished to hold him—with missions, commands, offices, pensions—all of which had to be lucrative and entail no work. The aristocracy remained loyal only because the king did precisely this. The large surplus beyond the requirements of debt service and administration which had existed at the outset of the era of Louis XIV, together with all the borrowings the crown was able to contrive—all this fell only nominally to the crown. Actually it had to be shared with the nobility which, in this fashion, received a pension from the pockets of the taxpayers.

A system of this kind was essentially untenable. It placed shackles of gold on real ability that sought outlet in action, bought up every natural opportunity for such talent to apply itself. There they were at Versailles, all these aristocrats—socially interned, consigned to amuse themselves under the monarch's gracious smile. There was absolutely nothing to do but to engage in flirtation, sports, and court festivities. These are fine pastimes, but they are life-filling only for relatively rare connoisseurs. Unless the nobles were to be allowed to revolt, they had to be kept busy. Now all the noble families whose members were amusing themselves at Versailles could look back on a warlike past, martial ideas and phrases, bellicose instincts. To ninety-nine out of a hundred of them, "action" meant military action. If civil war was to be avoided, then external wars were required. Foreign campaigns preoccupied and satisfied the nobility. From the viewpoint of the crown they were harmless and even advantageous. As it was, the crown was in control of the military machine, which must not be allowed to rust or languish. Tradition—as always surviving its usefulness—favored war as the natural pursuit of kings. And finally, the monarchy needed outward successes to maintain its position at home— how much it needed them was later shown when the pendulum swung to the other extreme, under Louis XV and Louis XVI. Small wonder that France took the field on every possible occasion, with an excess of enthusiasm that becomes wholly understandable from its position [1] and that left it quite indifferent to the actual nature of the occasion. Any war would do. If only there was war, the details of foreign policy were gladly left to the king.

Thus the belligerence and war policy of the autocratic state are explained from the necessities of its social structure, from the inherited dispositions of its ruling class, rather than from the immediate advantages to be derived by conquest. In calculating these advantages it is necessary to realize that possible gains to the bourgeoisie were not necessarily valid motives. For the king was in control of foreign policy, and bourgeois interests, on the whole rather impotent, weighed in the balance only when the king stood to gain by them. Certainly he stood to gain tax revenue when he promoted trade and commerce. But even then wars had already grown so costly that they might be doubtful risks to the king even though they offered indubitable advantages to business. Moreover, from the contemporary economic perspective—

which is the one that must be adopted—by no means all the undertakings of Louis XIV were calculated to promote commercial interests. On the contrary, he showed little discrimination, eagerly seizing both on plans asserted, sometimes falsely, to be commercially advantageous (such as the subjugation of the Netherlands), and on those for which no one put forward any such claim (such as the plan of the "reunions"). Indeed, the king actually showed a certain indifference toward commercial and colonial undertakings,[2] seeming to prefer small and fruitless undertakings in near-by Europe that appeared easy and promised success. The one man, incidentally, who, if anyone, should have been the driving power behind economically motivated wars, Colbert, was an avowed opponent of the war policy. It is time for the estimate of the share that mercantilism had in international military involvements at that time to be reduced to its proper dimensions. The theory that the wars of the late seventeenth and the eighteenth centuries were commercial wars does represent an advance over the superficial judgment of political history expressed in the phrase "cabinet wars"—which does not mean that that phrase lacks all significance—but the commercial theory involves considerable exaggeration. Industrial life was then only in its infancy. It was only just beginning to discard craft forms. Capital exports—which is the thing that would really be relevant in this connection—were quite out of the question, and even production was quantitatively so small that exports could not possibly occupy a central position in the policies of the state. Nor did they, in fact, occupy such a position. The monarchs may have been avaricious, but they were far too remote from commercial considerations to be governed by them. Even colonial questions impinged only slightly on the European policies of the great powers. Settlers and adventurers were often allowed to fight out such problems on the spot, and little attention was paid to them. That the basic theory of mercantilism was quite adequate to justify violent measures against foreign powers, and that in every war economic interests, as conceived by mercantilism, were safeguarded whenever possible—these facts tend to exaggerate the mercantilist element. Certainly it made a contribution. But industry was the servant of state policy to a greater degree than state policy served industry.

We do not seek to underestimate the immediate advantages, at the time, of an expansion of the national domain. This is an element that then had a significance much greater than it has today. At a time when communications were uncertain, making military protection of commerce necessary, every nation undoubtedly had an interest in national bases overseas as well as in Europe, and in colonies too, though not so much in the conquest of other European countries. Finally, for the absolute monarch conquest meant an increment in power, soldiers, and income. And had all the plans of Louis XIV succeeded, he would undoubtedly have "made a go of it." The inner necessity to engage in a policy of conquest was not distasteful to him. Yet that this element could play a part is explained only from the traditional habit of war and from the fact that the war machine stood ready at hand. Otherwise these instincts would have been inhibited, just as are predatory instincts in private life. Murder with intent to rob cannot be explained by the mere desire for the victim's money, any more than analogous suggestions explain the expansive policy of the absolutist state.

At the same time, it remains a peculiarity of this type of imperialism that the monarch's personal motives and interests are far more important to an understanding of its individual aspects than is true in the case of other types. The prince-become-state made foreign policy his own personal business and saw to it that it was the concern of no one else. His personal interests became the interests of the state. Hereditary claims, personal rancor and idiosyncrasy, family politics, individual generosity and similar traits cannot be denied a role as real factors shaping the surface situation. These things may have been no more than individual manifestations of a social situation, social data processed through an individual temperament; but superficially, at least, they aid make history to the extent that they, in turn, had consequences that became elements of the social situation. It was this period that gave rise to the notion, so deeply rooted in the popular mind down to recent times, that foreign policy can be explained by the whims of sovereigns and their relations to one another. It gave rise to the whole approach that judges events from the viewpoint of monarchial interest, honor, and morality—an approach stemming directly from the social views of the time (as seen, for example, in the letters of Mme. de Sevigné) and one that adapts itself only slowly to changing times.

Invaluable evidence in this respect is furnished by the memoirs of Frederick the Great, mainly because his keen mind analyzed itself with far less prejudice than our Assyrian king ever did. In all cases of this kind the psychological aspects were surely determined by the desire to shine, to play an important role, to become the cynosure of discussion, to exploit existing power resources—all the while pursuing one's own advantage. Tradition and the availability of appropriate means are entirely sufficient to explain why these motives tended toward war. Domestic contingencies were subordinate, for in Germany, at least, the sovereign had triumphed over the nobility to such an extent that little political effort was required in that direction. The farther east we go, the more completely we see the sovereign able to regard state and people as his private property—with the noteworthy exception of Hungary, which can be compared only with England. The absolute monarch who can do as he pleases, who wages war in the same way as he rides to hounds—to satisfy his need for action—such is the face of absolutist imperialism.

The character of such absolutism is nowhere plainer than in Russia, notably the Russia of Catherine II. The case is particularly interesting because the Slavic masses never have shown and do not now show the slightest trace of militancy or aggressiveness. This has been true ever since the distant past, the time of settlement in the swamplands of the Pripet. It is true that the Slavs soon mingled with Germanic and

Mongol elements and that their empire soon embraced a number of warlike peoples. But there never was any question of imperialist trends on the part of the Russian peasant or worker. Triumphant czarism rested on those Germanic and Mongol elements, elaborated its empire, created its army, without essentially impinging on the sphere of the peasant except to levy taxes and recruits for the army. In the time of feudalism as well as later, after the liberation of the peasants, we have the singular picture of a peasant democracy—one that was at times sorely oppressed by the nobility, but on which a bureaucratic and military despotism was superimposed in only superficial fashion. Once this despotism was securely established—and this occurred definitively under Peter the Great—it immediately exhibited that trend toward limitless expansion which our theory readily explains from the objectless "momentum of the machine in motion," the urge to action of a ruling class disposed to war, the concern of the crown to maintain its prestige—but which becomes quite incomprehensible to any rational approach from existing interests. Such interests—that is, those springing from vital needs—ceased to exist in the case of Russia from the moment that access to the Baltic and the Black Seas was won. This is so obvious that the argument of vital interest has not even been put forward. Instead, *ex post* explanations have been concocted, both inside Russia and out, which have gained considerable credence and are held to be verified by the otherwise unexplained tendencies to expansion—an example of reasoning in a circle, by no means uncommon in the social sciences. Among the motives thus postulated are the urge for Pan-Slav unification, the desire to liberate the Christian world from the Mohammedan yoke—even a mystical yearning for Constantinople on the part of the Russian people! And as often happens when such analysis encounters difficulties, refuge is sought in the allegedly bottomless depths of the "national soul." Actually, the continued momentum of acquired forms of life and organization, fostered by domestic interests, is entirely adequate to explain the policies of, say, Catherine II. True, from the subjective viewpoint a war policy undoubtedly recommended itself to her as the natural outcome of tradition, and, in addition, presumably as an interesting toy. Moreover, there was the example of the great lords whom she was copying. War was part of their settled order of life, so to speak—an element of sovereign splendor, almost a fashion. Hence they waged war whenever the occasion was offered, not so much from considerations of advantage as from personal whim. To look for deep-laid plans, broad perspectives, consistent trends is to miss the whole point.

IMPERIALISM AND CAPITALISM

Our analysis of the historical evidence has shown, first, the unquestionable fact that "objectless" tendencies toward forcible expansion, without definite, utilitarian limits—that is, non-rational and irrational, purely instinctual inclinations toward war and conquest—play a very large role in the history of mankind. It may sound paradoxical, but numberless wars —perhaps the majority of all wars—have been waged without adequate "reason"—not so much from the moral viewpoint as from that of reasoned and reasonable interest. The most herculean efforts of the nations, in other words, have faded into the empty air.[1] Our analysis, in the second place, provides an explanation for this drive to action, this will to war—a theory by no means exhausted by mere references to an "urge" or an "instinct." The explanation lies, instead, in the vital needs of situations that molded peoples and classes into warriors—if they wanted to avoid extinction—and in the fact that psychological dispositions and social structures acquired in the dim past in such situations, once firmly established, tend to maintain themselves and to continue in effect long after they have lost their meaning and their life-preserving function. Our analysis, in the third place, has shown the existence of subsidiary factors that facilitate the survival of such dispositions and structures—factors that may be divided into two groups. The orientation toward war is mainly fostered by the domestic interests of ruling classes, but also by the influence of all those who stand to gain individually from a war policy, whether economically or socially. Both groups of factors are generally overgrown by elements of an altogether different character, not only in terms of political phraseology, but also of psychological motivation. Imperialisms differ greatly in detail, but they all have at least these traits in common, turning them into a single phenomenon in the field of sociology, as we noted in the introduction.

Imperialism thus is atavistic in character. It falls into that large group of surviving features from earlier ages that play such an important part in every concrete social situation. In other words, it is an element that stems from the living conditions, not of the present, but of the past—or, put in terms of the economic interpretation of history, from past rather than present relations of production.[2] It is an atavism in the social structure, in individual, psychological habits of emotional reaction. Since the vital needs that created it have passed away for good, it too must gradually disappear, even though every warlike involvement, no matter how non-imperialist in character, tends to revive it. It tends to disappear as a structural element because the structure that brought it to the fore goes into a decline, giving way, in the course of social development, to other structures that have no room for it and eliminate the power factors that supported it. It tends to disappear as an element of habitual emotional reaction, because of the progressive rationalization of life and mind, a process in which old functional needs are absorbed by new tasks, in which heretofore military energies are functionally modified. If our theory is correct, cases of imperialism should decline in intensity the later they occur in the history of a people and of a culture. Our most recent examples of unmistakable, clear-cut imperialism are the absolute monarchies of the eighteenth century. They are unmistakably "more civilized" than their predecessors.

It is from absolute autocracy that the present age has taken over what imperialist tendencies it displays. And the imperialism of absolute autocracy flourished before the Industrial Revolution that created the modern world, or rather, before the consequences of that revolution began to be felt in all their aspects. These two statements are primarily meant in a historical sense, and as such they are no more than self-evident. We shall nevertheless try, within the framework of our theory, to define the significance of capitalism for our phenomenon and to examine the relationship between present-day imperialist tendencies and the autocratic imperialism of the eighteenth century.

The floodtide that burst the dams in the Industrial Revolution had its sources, of course, back in the Middle Ages. But capitalism began to shape society and impress its stamp on every page of social history only with the second half of the eighteenth century. Before that time there had been only islands of capitalist economy imbedded in an ocean of village and urban economy. True, certain political influences emanated from these islands, but they were able to assert themselves only indirectly. Not until the process we term the Industrial Revolution did the working masses, led by the entrepreneur, overcome the bonds of older life-forms—the environment of peasantry, guild, and aristocracy. The causal connection was this: a transformation in the basic economic factors (which need not detain us here) created the objective opportunity for the production of commodities, for large-scale industry, working for a market of customers whose individual identities were unknown, operating solely with a view to maximum financial profit. It was this opportunity that created an economically oriented leadership—personalities whose field of achievement was the organization of such commodity production in the form of capitalist enterprise. Successful enterprises in large numbers represented something new in the economic and social sense. They fought for and won freedom of action. They compelled state policy to adapt itself to their needs. More and more they attracted the most vigorous leaders from other spheres, as well as the manpower of those spheres, causing them and the social strata they represented to languish. Capitalist entrepreneurs fought the former ruling circles for a share in state control, for leadership in the state. The very fact of their success, their position, their resources, their power, raised them in the political and social scale. Their mode of life, their cast of mind became increasingly important elements on the social scene. Their actions, desires, needs, and beliefs emerged more and more sharply within the total picture of the social community. In a historical sense, this applied primarily to the industrial and financial leaders of the movement—the bourgeoisie. But soon it applied also to the working masses which this movement created and placed in an altogether new class situation. This situation was governed by new forms of the working day, of family life, of interests—and these, in turn, corresponded to new orientations toward the social structure as a whole. More and more, in the course of the nineteenth century, the typical modern worker came to determine the over-all aspect of society; for competitive capitalism, by its inherent logic, kept on raising the demand for labor and thus the economic level and social power of the workers,[3] until this class too was able to assert itself in a political sense. The working class and its mode of life provided the type from which the intellectual developed. Capitalism did not create the intellectuals—the "new middle class." But in earlier times only the legal scholar, the cleric, and the physician had formed a special intellectual class, and even they had enjoyed but little scope for playing an independent role. Such opportunities were provided only by capitalist society, which created the industrial and financial bureaucrat, the journalist, and so on, and which opened up new vistas to the jurist and physician. The "professional" of capitalist society arose as a class type. Finally, as a class type, the rentier, the beneficiary of industrial loan capital, is also a creature of capitalism. All these types are shaped by the capitalist mode of production, and they tend for this reason to bring other types—even the peasant—into conformity with themselves.

These new types were now cast adrift from the fixed order of earlier times, from the environment that had shackled and protected people for centuries, from the old associations of village, manor house, clan fellowship, often even from families in the broader sense. They were severed from the things that had been constant year after year, from cradle to grave—tools, homes, the countryside, especially the soil. They were on their own, enmeshed in the pitiless logic of gainful employment, mere drops in the vast ocean of industrial life, exposed to the inexorable pressures of competition. They were freed from the control of ancient patterns of thought, of the grip of institutions and organs that taught and represented these outlooks in village, manor, and guild. They were removed from the old world, engaged in building a new one for themselves—a specialized, mechanized world. Thus they were all inevitably democratized, individualized, and rationalized.[4] They were democratized, because the picture of time-honored power and privilege gave way to one of continual change, set in motion by industrial life. They were individualized, because subjective opportunities to shape their lives took the place of immutable objective factors. They were rationalized, because the instability of economic position made their survival hinge on continual, deliberately rationalistic decisions—a dependence that emerged with great sharpness. Trained to economic rationalism, these people left no sphere of life unrationalized, questioning everything about themselves, the social structure, the state, the ruling class. The marks of this process are engraved on every aspect of modern culture. It is this process that explains the basic features of that culture.

These are things that are well known today, recognized in their full significance—indeed, often exaggerated. Their application to our subject is plain. Everything that is purely instinctual, everything insofar as it is purely instinctual, is driven into the background by this development. It creates a social and psychological atmosphere in keeping with modern economic forms, where traditional habits, merely because they were traditional, could no more survive than obsolete economic forms. Just as the latter can survive only if they are continually "adapted," so instinctual tendencies can survive only when the conditions that gave rise to them continue to apply, or when the "instinct" in question derives a new purpose from new conditions. The "instinct" that is *only* "instinct," that has lost its purpose, languishes relatively quickly in the capitalist world, just as does an inefficient economic practice. We see this process of rationalization at work even in the case of the strongest impulses. We observe it, for example, in the facts of procreation. We must therefore anticipate finding it in the case of the imperialist impulse as well; we must expect to see this impulse, which rests on the primitive contingencies of physical combat, gradually disappear, washed away by new exigencies of daily life. There is another factor too. The competitive system absorbs the full energies of most of the people at all economic levels. Constant application, attention, and concentration of energy are the conditions of survival within it, primarily in the specifically economic professions, but also in other activities organized on their model. There is much less excess energy to be vented in war and conquest than in any precapitalist society. What excess energy there is flows largely into industry itself, accounts for its shining figures—the type of the captain of industry—and for the rest is applied to art, science, and the social struggle. In a purely capitalist world, what was once energy for war becomes simply energy for labor of every kind. Wars of conquest and adventurism in foreign policy in general are bound to be regarded as troublesome distractions, destructive of life's meaning, a diversion from the accustomed and therefore "true" task.

A purely capitalist world therefore can offer no fertile soil to imperialist impulses. That does not mean that it cannot still maintain an interest in imperialist expansion. We shall discuss this immediately. The point is that its people are likely to be essentially of an unwarlike disposition. Hence we must expect that anti-imperialist tendencies will show themselves wherever capitalism penetrates the economy and, through the economy, the mind of modern nations—most strongly, of course, where capitalism itself is strongest, where it has advanced furthest, encountered the least resistance, and preeminently where its types and hence democracy—in the "bourgeois" sense—come closest to political dominion. We must further expect that the types formed by capitalism will actually be the carriers of these tendencies. Is such the case? The facts that follow are cited to show that this expectation, which flows from our theory, is in fact justified.

1. Throughout the world of capitalism, and specifically among the elements formed by capitalism in modern social life, there has arisen a fundamental opposition to war, expansion, cabinet diplomacy, armaments, and socially entrenched professional armies. This opposition had its origin in the country that first turned capitalist—England—and arose coincidentally with that country's capitalist development. "Philosophical radicalism" was the first politically influential intellectual movement to represent this trend successfully, linking it up, as was to be expected, with economic freedom in general and free trade in particular. Molesworth became a cabinet member, even though he had publicly declared— on the occasion of the Canadian revolution—that he prayed for the defeat of his country's arms. In step with the advance of capitalism,[5] the movement also gained adherents elsewhere—though at first only adherents without influence. It found support in Paris—indeed, in a circle oriented toward capitalist enterprise (for example, Frédéric Passy). True, pacifism as a matter of principle had existed before, though only among a few small religious sects. But modern pacifism, in its political foundations if not its derivation, is unquestionably a phenomenon of the capitalist world.

2. Wherever capitalism penetrated, peace parties of such strength arose that virtually every war meant a political struggle on the domestic scene. The exceptions are rare— Germany in the Franco-Prussian war of 1870-1871, both belligerents in the Russo-Turkish war of 1877-1878. That is

why every war is carefully justified as a defensive war by the governments involved, and by all the political parties, in their official utterances—indicating a realization that a war of a different nature would scarcely be tenable in a political sense. (Here too the Russo-Turkish war is an exception, but a significant one.) In former times this would not have been necessary. Reference to an interest or pretense at moral justification was customary as early as the eighteenth century, but only in the nineteenth century did the assertion of attack, or the threat of attack, become the only avowed occasion for war. In the distant past, imperialism had needed no disguise whatever, and in the absolute autocracies only a very transparent one; but today imperialism is carefully hidden from public view—even though there may still be an unofficial appeal to warlike instincts. No people and no ruling class today can openly afford to regard war as a normal state of affairs or a normal element in the life of nations. No one doubts that today it must be characterized as an abnormality and a disaster. True, war is still glorified. But glorification in the style of King Tuglâtî-palisharra is rare and unleashes such a storm of indignation that every practical politician carefully dissociates himself from such things. Everywhere there is official acknowledgment that peace is an end in itself—though not necessarily an end overshadowing all purposes that can be realized by means of war. Every expansionist urge must be carefully related to a concrete goal. All this is primarily a matter of political phraseology, to be sure. But the necessity for this phraseology is a symptom of the popular attitude. And that attitude makes a policy of imperialism more and more difficult—indeed, the very word imperialism is applied only to the enemy, in a reproachful sense, being carefully avoided with reference to the speaker's own policies.

3. The type of industrial worker created by capitalism is always vigorously anti-imperialist. In the individual case, skillful agitation may persuade the working masses to approve or remain neutral—a concrete goal or interest in self-defense always playing the main part—but no initiative for

a forcible policy of expansion ever emanates from this quarter. On this point official socialism unquestionably formulates not merely the interests but also the conscious will of the workers. Even less than peasant imperialism is there any such thing as socialist or other working-class imperialism.

4. Despite manifest resistance on the part of powerful elements, the capitalist age has seen the development of methods for preventing war, for the peaceful settlement of disputes among states. The very fact of resistance means that the trend can be explained only from the mentality of capitalism as a mode of life. It definitely limits the opportunities imperialism needs if it is to be a powerful force. True, the methods in question often fail, but even more often they are successful. I am thinking not merely of the Hague Court of Arbitration but of the practice of submitting controversial issues to conferences of the major powers or at least those powers directly concerned—a course of action that has become less and less avoidable. True, here too the individual case may become a farce. But the serious setbacks of today must not blind us to the real importance or sociological significance of these things.

5. Among all capitalist economies, that of the United States is least burdened with precapitalist elements, survivals, reminiscences, and power factors. Certainly we cannot expect to find imperialist tendencies altogether lacking even in the United States, for the immigrants came from Europe with their convictions fully formed, and the environment certainly favored the revival of instincts of pugnacity. But we can conjecture that among all countries the United States is likely to exhibit the weakest imperialist trend. This turns out to be the truth. The case is particularly instructive, because the United States has seen a particularly strong emergence of capitalist interests in an imperialist direction— those very interests to which the phenomenon of imperialism has so often been reduced, a subject we shall yet touch on. Nevertheless the United States was the first advocate of disarmament and arbitration. It was the first to conclude treaties concerning arms limitations (1817) and arbitral courts

(first attempt in 1797)—doing so most zealously, by the way. when economic interest in expansion was at its greatest. Since 1908 such treaties have been concluded with twenty-two states. In the course of the nineteenth century, the United States had numerous occasions for war, including instances that were well calculated to test its patience. It made almost no use of such occasions. Leading industrial and financial circles in the United States had and still have an evident interest in incorporating Mexico into the Union. There was more than enough opportunity for such annexation—but Mexico remained unconquered. Racial catch phrases and working-class interests pointed to Japan as a possible danger. Hence possession of the Philippines was not a matter of indifference—yet surrender of this possession is being discussed. Canada was an almost defenseless prize—but Canada remained independent. Even in the United States, of course, politicians need slogans—especially slogans calculated to divert attention from domestic issues. Theodore Roosevelt and certain magnates of the press actually resorted to imperialism—and the result, in that world of high capitalism, was utter defeat, a defeat that would have been even more abject, if other slogans, notably those appealing to anti-trust sentiment, had not met with better success.[6]

These facts are scarcely in dispute.[7] And since they fit into the picture of the mode of life which we have recognized to be the necessary product of capitalism, since we can grasp them adequately from the necessities of that mode of life and industry, it follows that capitalism is by nature anti-imperialist. Hence we cannot readily derive from it such imperialist tendencies as actually exist, but must evidently see them only as alien elements, carried into the world of capitalism from the outside, supported by non-capitalist factors in modern life. The survival of interest in a policy of forcible expansion does not, by itself, alter these facts—not even, it must be steadily emphasized, from the viewpoint of the economic interpretation of history. For objective interests become effective—and, what is important, become powerful political factors—only when they correspond to attitudes of the people or of sufficiently powerful strata. Otherwise they remain without effect, are not even conceived of as interests. The economic interest in the forcible conquest of India had to await free-booter personalities, in order to be followed up. In ancient Rome the domestic class interest in an expansive policy had to be seized upon by a vigorous, idle aristocracy, otherwise it would have been ruled out on internal political grounds. Even the purely commercial imperialism of Venice—assuming that we can speak of such a thing, and not merely of a policy of securing trade routes in a military sense, which was then necessary—even such a policy needed to have examples of a policy of conquest at hand on every side, needed mercenary groups and bellicose adventurers among the *nobili* in order to become true imperialism. The capitalist world, however, suppresses rather than creates such attitudes. Certainly, all expansive interests within it are likely to ally themselves with imperialist tendencies flowing from non-capitalist sources, to use them, to make them serve as pretexts, to rationalize them, to point the way toward action on account of them. And from this union the picture of modern imperialism is put together; but for that very reason it is not a matter of capitalist factors alone. Before we go into this at length, we must understand the nature and strength of the economic stake which capitalist society has in a policy of imperialism—especially the question of whether this interest is or is not inherent in the nature of capitalism—either capitalism generally, or a special phase of capitalism.

It is in the nature of a capitalist economy—and of an exchange economy generally—that many people stand to gain economically in any war. Here the situation is fundamentally much as it is with the familiar subject of luxury. War means increased demand at panic prices, hence high profits and also high wages in many parts of the national economy. This is primarily a matter of money incomes, but as a rule (though to a lesser extent) real incomes are also affected. There are, for example, the special war interests, such as the arms industry. If the war lasts long enough, the circle of money profiteers naturally expands more and more—quite apart from a possible paper-money economy. It may extend to every economic field, but just as naturally the commodity content of money profits drops more and more, indeed, quite rapidly, to the point where actual losses are incurred. The national economy as a whole, of course, is impoverished by the tremendous excess in consumption brought on by war. It is, to be sure, conceivable that either the capitalists or the workers might make certain gains as a class, namely, if the volume either of capital or of labor should decline in such a way that the remainder receives a greater share in the social product and that, even from the absolute viewpoint, the total sum of interest or wages becomes greater than it was before. But these advantages cannot be considerable. They are probably, for the most part, more than outweighed by the burdens imposed by war and by losses sustained abroad. Thus the gain of the capitalists as a class cannot be a motive for war—and it is this gain that counts, for any advantage to the working class would be contingent on a large number of workers falling in action or otherwise perishing. There remain the entrepreneurs in the war industries, in the broader sense, possibly also the large landowner—a small but powerful minority. Their war profits are always sure to be an important supporting element. But few will go so far as to assert that this element alone is sufficient to orient the people of the capitalist world along imperialist lines. At most, an interest in expansion may make the capitalists allies of those who stand for imperialist trends.

It may be stated as being beyond controversy that where free trade prevails *no* class has an interest in forcible expansion as such. For in such a case the citizens and goods of every nation can move in foreign countries as freely as though those countries were politically their own—free trade implying far more than mere freedom from tariffs. In a genuine state of free trade, foreign raw materials and foodstuffs are as accessible to each nation as though they were within its own territory.[8] Where the cultural backwardness of a region makes normal economic intercourse dependent on colonization, it does not matter, assuming free trade, which of the "civilized" nations undertakes the task of colonization. Dominion of the seas, in such a case, means little more than a maritime traffic police. Similarly, it is a matter of indifference to a nation whether a railway concession in a foreign country is acquired by one of its own citizens or not—just so long as the railway *is* built and put into efficient operation. For citizens of any country may use the railway, just like the fellow countrymen of its builder— while in the event of war it will serve whoever controls it in the military sense, regardless of who built it. It is true, of course, that profits and wages flowing from its construction and operation will accrue, for the greater part, to the nation that built it. But capital and labor that go into the railway have to be taken from somewhere, and normally the other nations fill the gap. It is a fact that in a regime of free trade the essential advantages of international intercourse are clearly evident. The gain lies in the enlargement of the commodity supply by means of the division of labor among nations, rather than in the profits and wages of the export industry and the carrying trade. For these profits and wages would be reaped even if there were no export, in which case import, the necessary complement, would also vanish. Not even monopoly interests—if they existed—would be disposed toward imperialism in such a case. For under free trade only *international* cartels would be possible. Under a system of free trade there would be conflicts in economic interest neither among different nations nor among the corresponding classes of different nations.[9] And since protectionism is not an essential characteristic of the capitalist economy—otherwise the English national economy would scarcely be capitalist—it is apparent that any economic interest in forcible expansion on the part of a people or a class is not necessarily a product of capitalism.

Protective tariffs alone—and harassment of the alien and of foreign commodities—do not basically change this situation as it affects interests. True, such barriers move the nations economically farther apart, making it easier for imperialist tendencies to win the upper hand; they line up the entrepreneurs of the different countries in battle formation against one another, impeding the rise of peaceful interests; they also hinder the flow of raw materials and foodstuffs and thus the export of manufactures, or conversely, the import of manufactures and the export of raw materials and foodstuffs, possibly creating an interest in—sometimes forcible—expansion of the customs area; they place entrepreneurs in a position of dependence on regulations of governments that may be serving imperialist interests, giving these governments occasion to pervert economic relations for purposes of sharpening economic conflicts, for adulterating the competitive struggle with diplomatic methods outside the field of economics, and, finally, for imposing on people the heavy sacrifices exacted by a policy of autarchy, thus accustoming them to the thought of war by constant preparation for war. Nevertheless, in this case the basic alignment of interests remains essentially what it was under free trade. We might reiterate our example of railway construction, though in the case of mining concessions, for example, the situation is somewhat different. Colonial possessions acquire more meaning in this case, but the exclusion from the colonies of aliens and foreign capital is not altogether good business since it slows down the development of the colonies. The same is true of the struggle for third markets. When, for example, France obtains more favorable tariff treatment from the Chinese government than England enjoys, this will avail only those French exporters who are in a position to export the same goods as their English confrères; the others are only harmed. It is true, of course, that protectionism adds another form of international capital movement to the kind that prevails under free trade—or rather, a modification of it—namely, the movement of capital for the founding of enterprises inside the tariff wall, in order to save customs duties. But this capital movement too has no aggressive element; on the contrary, it tends toward the creation of peaceful interests. Thus an aggressive economic policy on the part of a country with a unified tariff—with preparedness for war always in the background—serves the economy only seemingly rather than really. Actually, one might assert that the economy becomes a weapon in the political struggle, a means for unifying the nation, for severing it from the fabric of international interests, for placing it at the disposal of the state power.

This becomes especially clear when we consider which strata of the capitalist world are actually economically benefited by protective tariffs. They do harm to both workers and capitalists—in contrast to entrepreneurs—not only in their role as consumers, but also as producers. The damage to consumers is universal, that to producers almost so. As for entrepreneurs, they are benefited only by the tariff that happens to be levied on their own product. But this advantage is substantially reduced by the countermeasures adopted by other countries—universally, except in the case of England—and by the effect of the tariff on the prices of other articles, especially those which they require for their own productive process. Why, then, are entrepreneurs so strongly in favor of protective tariffs? The answer is simple. Each industry hopes to score *special* gains in the struggle of political intrigue, thus enabling it to realize a net gain. Moreover, every decline in freight rates, every advance in production abroad, is likely to affect the economic balance, making it necessary for domestic enterprises to adapt themselves, indeed often to turn to other lines of endeavor. This is a difficult task to which not everyone is equal. Within the industrial organism of every nation there survive antiquated methods of doing business that would cause enterprises to succumb to foreign competition—because of poor management rather than lack of capital, for before 1914 the banks were almost forcing capital on the entrepreneurs.[10] If, still, in most countries virtually *all* entrepreneurs are protectionists, this is owing to a reason which we shall presently discuss. Without that reason, their attitude would be different. The fact that all industries today demand tariff protection must not blind us to the fact that even the entrepreneur interest is not unequivocally protectionist. For this demand is only the consequence of a protectionism already in existence, of a protectionist spirit springing from the economic interests of relatively small entrepreneur groups and from non-capitalist elements—a spirit that ultimately carried along all groups, occasionally even the representatives of working-class interests. Today the protective tariff confers its full and immediate benefits—or comes close to conferring them—only on the large landowners.

A protectionist policy, however, does facilitate the formation of cartels and trusts. And it is true that this circumstance thoroughly alters the alignment of interests. It was neo-Marxist doctrine that first tellingly described this causal connection (Bauer) and fully recognized the significance of the "functional change in protectionism" (Hilferding). Union in a cartel or trust confers various benefits on the entrepreneur—a saving in costs, a stronger position as against the workers—but none of these compares with this one advantage: a monopolistic price policy, possible to any considerable degree *only* behind an adequate protective tariff. Now the price that brings the maximum monopoly profit is generally far above the price that would be fixed by fluctuating competitive costs, and the volume that can be marketed at that maximum price is generally far below the output that would be technically and economically feasible. Under free competition that output *would* be produced and offered, but a trust cannot offer it, for it could be sold only at a competitive price. Yet the trust *must* produce it—or approximately as much—otherwise the advantages of large-scale enterprise remain unexploited and unit costs are likely to be uneconomically high. The trust thus faces a dilemma. Either it renounces the monopolistic policies that motivated its founding; or it fails to exploit and expand its plant, with resultant high costs. It extricates itself from this dilemma by producing the full output that is economically feasible, thus securing low costs, and offering in the protected domestic market only the quantity corresponding to the monopoly price—insofar as the tariff permits; while the rest is sold, or "dumped," abroad at a lower price, sometimes (but not necessarily) *below* cost.

What happens when the entrepreneurs successfully pursue such a policy is something that did not occur in the cases discussed so far—a conflict of interests between nations that becomes so sharp that it cannot be overcome by the existing basic community of interests. Each of the two groups of entrepreneurs and each of the two states seeks to do something that is rendered illusory by a similar policy on the part of the other. In the case of protective tariffs *without* monopoly formation, an understanding is sometimes possible, for only a few would be destroyed, while many would stand to gain; but when monopoly rules it is very difficult to reach an agreement for it would require self-negation on the part of the new rulers. All that is left to do is to pursue the course once taken, to beat down the foreign industry wherever possible, forcing it to conclude a favorable "peace." This requires sacrifices. The excess product is dumped on the world market at steadily lower prices. Counterattacks that grow more and more desperate must be repulsed on the domestic scene. The atmosphere grows more and more heated. Workers and consumers grow more and more troublesome. Where this situation prevails, capital export, like commodity export, becomes aggressive, belying its ordinary character. A mass of capitalists competing with one another has no means of counteracting the decline in the interest rate. Of course they always seek out the places where the interest rate is highest, and in this quest they are quite willing to export their capital. But they are unable to adopt a policy of forced capital exports; and where there is freedom of capital movement they also lack the motive. For any gaps which might be opened up at home would be filled by foreign capital flowing in from abroad, thus preventing a rise of the domestic interest rate. But *organized* capital may very well make the discovery that the interest rate can be maintained above the level of free competition, if the resulting surplus can be sent abroad and if any foreign capital that flows in can be intercepted and—whether in the form of loans or in the form of machinery and the like—can likewise be channeled into foreign investment outlets. Now it is true that capital is nowhere cartelized. But it is everywhere subject to the guidance of the big banks which, even without a capital cartel, have attained a position similar to that of the cartel magnates in industry, and which are in a position to put into effect similar policies. It is necessary to keep two factors in mind. In the first place, everywhere except, significantly, in England, there has come into being a close alliance between high finance and the cartel magnates, often going as far as personal identity. Although the relation between capitalists and entrepreneurs is one of the typical and fundamental *conflicts* of the capitalist economy, monopoly capitalism has virtually fused the big banks and cartels into one. Leading bankers are often leaders of the national economy. Here capitalism has found a central organ that supplants its automatism by conscious decisions. In the second place, the interests of the big banks coincide with those of their depositors even less than do the interests of cartel leaders with those of the firms belonging to the cartel. The policies of high finance are based on control of a *large* proportion of the national capital, but they are in the actual interest of only a *small* proportion and, indeed, with respect to the alliance with big business, sometimes not even in the interest of capital as such at all. The ordinary "small" capitalist foots the bills for a policy of forced exports, rather than enjoying its profits. He is a tool; his interests do not really matter. This possibility of laying all the sacrifices connected with a monopoly policy on one part of capital, while removing them from another, makes capital exports far more lucrative for the favored part than they would otherwise be. Even capital that is independent of the banks is thus often forced abroad—forced into the role of a shock troop for the real leaders, because cartels successfully impede the founding of new enterprises. Thus the customs area of a trustified country generally pours a huge wave of capital into new countries. There it meets other, similar waves of capital, and a bitter, costly struggle begins but never ends.

In such a struggle among "dumped" products and capitals, it is no longer a matter of indifference who builds a given railroad, who owns a mine or a colony. Now that the law of costs is no longer operative, it becomes necessary to fight over such properties with desperate effort and with every available means, including those that are not economic in character, such as diplomacy. The concrete objects in question often become entirely subsidiary considerations; the anticipated profit may be trifling, because of the competitive struggle—a struggle that has very little to do with normal competition. What matters is to gain a foothold of some kind and then to exploit this foothold as a base for the conquest of new markets. This costs all the participants dear—often more than can be reasonably recovered, immediately or in the future. Fury lays hold of everyone concerned—and everyone sees to it that his fellow countrymen share his wrath. Each is constrained to resort to methods that he would regard as evidence of unprecedented moral depravity in the other.

It is not true that the capitalist system as such must collapse from immanent necessity, that it necessarily makes its continued existence impossible by its own growth and development. Marx's line of reasoning on this point shows serious defects, and when these are corrected the proof vanishes. It is to the great credit of Hilferding that he abandoned this thesis of Marxist theory.[11] Nevertheless, the situation that has just been described is really untenable both politically and economically. Economically, it amounts to a *reductio ad absurdum*. Politically, it unleashes storms of indignation among the exploited consumers at home and the threatened producers abroad. Thus the idea of military force readily suggests itself. Force may serve to break down foreign customs barriers and thus afford relief from the vicious circle of economic aggression. If that is not feasible, military conquest may at least secure control over markets in which heretofore one had to compete with the enemy. In this context, the conquest of colonies takes on an altogether different significance. Non-monopolist countries, especially those adhering to free trade, reap little profit from such a policy. But it is a different matter with countries that function in a monopolist role *vis-à-vis* their colonies. There being no competition, they can use cheap native labor without its ceasing to be cheap; they can market their products, even in the colonies, at monopoly prices; they can, finally, invest capital that would only depress the profit rate at home and that could be placed in other civilized countries only at very low interest rates. And they can do all these things even though the consequence may be much slower colonial development. It would seem as though there could be no such interest in expansion at the expense of other advanced capitalist countries—in Europe, for example—because their industry would merely offer competition to the domestic cartels. But it is sufficient for the industry of the conquering state to be superior to that of the one to be subjugated—superior in capital power, organization, intelligence, and self-assertion— to make it possible to treat the subjugated state, perhaps not quite, but very much like a colony, even though it may become necessary to make a deal with individual groups of interests that are particularly powerful. A much more important fact is that the conqueror can face the subjugated nation with the hearing of the victor. He has countless means at his disposal for expropriating raw material resources and the like and placing them in the service of his cartels. He can seize them outright, nationalize them, impose a forced sale, or draft the proprietors into industrial groups of the victor nation under conditions that insure control by the domestic captains of industry. He can exploit them by a system of quotas or allotments. He can administer the conquered means of communication in the interests of his own cartels. Under the pretext of military and political security, he can deprive the foreign workers of the right to organize, thus not only making cheap labor in the annexed territory available to his cartels, but also holding a threat over the head of domestic labor.

Thus we have here, within a social group that carries great political weight, a strong, undeniable, economic interest in such things as protective tariffs, cartels, monopoly prices, forced exports (dumping), an aggressive economic policy, an aggressive foreign policy generally, and war, including wars of expansion with a typically imperialist character. Once this alignment of interests exists, an even stronger interest in a somewhat differently motivated expansion must be added, namely, an interest in the conquest of lands producing raw materials and foodstuffs, with a view to facilitating self-sufficient warfare. Still another interest is that in rising wartime consumption. A mass of unorganized capitalists competing with one another may at best reap a trifling profit from such an eventuality, but organized capital is sure to profit hugely. Finally there is the political interest in war and international hatred which flows from the insecure position of the leading circles. They are small in numbers and highly unpopular. The essential nature of their policy is quite generally known, and most of the people find it unnatural and contemptible. An attack on all forms of property has revolutionary implications, but an attack on the privileged position of the cartel magnates may be politically rewarding, implying comparatively little risk and no threat to the existing order. Under certain circumstances it may serve to unite all the political parties. The existence of such a danger calls for diversionary tactics.

Yet the final word in any presentation of this aspect of modern economic life must be one of warning against overestimating it. The conflicts that have been described, born of an export-dependent monopoly capitalism, may serve to submerge the real community of interests among nations; the monopolist press may drive it underground; but underneath the surface it never completely disappears. Deep down, the normal sense of business and trade usually prevails. Even cartels cannot do without the custom of their foreign economic kin. Even national economies characterized by export monopoly are dependent on one another in many respects. And their interests do not always conflict in the matter of producing for third markets. Even when the conflicting interests are emphasized, parallel interests are not altogether lacking. Furthermore, if a policy of export monopolism is to be driven to the extremes of forcible expansion, it is necessary to win over all segments of the population—at least to the point where they are halfway prepared to support the war; but the real interest in export monopolism as such is limited to the entrepreneurs and their ally, high finance. Even the most skillful agitation cannot prevent the independent traders, the small producers who are not covered by cartels, the "mere" capitalists, and the workers from occasionally realizing that they are the victims of such a policy. In the case of the traders and small producers this is quite clear. It is not so clear in the case of the capitalists, because of the possibility of "dumping" capital in order to raise the domestic interest rate. Against this, however, stands the high cost of such a policy and the curtailment of the competition of entrepreneurs for domestic capital. It is of the greatest importance, finally, to understand that export monopolism injures the workers far more unequivocally than the capitalists. There can be no dumping of labor power, and employment abroad or in the colonies is not even a quantitative substitute. Curiously enough, this injury to the working class is a matter of controversy. Even neo-Marxist doctrine—and not merely those writers properly characterized as "vulgar Marxists," who in every respect resemble their ilk of other persuasions—is inclined to admit that the workers derive temporary benefits from export monopolism,[12] limiting the polemic against it to proof that the ultimate effects—economic and especially political—are doubtful, and that even the temporary benefits are purchased by an injury to foreign workers which conflicts with the spirit of socialism. There is an error here. Apparently it is assumed that production for export—and, to the extent that it fosters such production, monopoly capitalist expansion as well—increases the demand for labor and thus raises wages. Suppose we accept as correct the premises implied in this argument, that the increase in demand will outweigh any decrease flowing from monopolistic labor-saving production methods, and also that it will outweigh the disadvantage flowing from the fact that the workers are now confronted, rather than by many entrepreneurs in a single industry, by a single party of the second part who, on the local labor market at least, can engage in monopolistic policies with respect to them, both as workers and as consumers. Even if we accept these premises—which seem doubtful to me—the balance is not even temporarily in favor of the workers. We have already pointed out that the interest of workers in export, even when free trade prevails, is essentially a consumer interest; that is, it is based on the fact that exports make imports possible. But as a producer the worker will usually fare no worse without exports, since the lack of exports must also eliminate imports. The workers, moreover, have no interest whatever in exports that may result from a policy of export monopolism—in other words, that would not otherwise be exported at all. For if it were impossible to dump these quantities they would by no means remain unproduced. On the contrary, most, if not all, would be offered at home, in general affording the same employment opportunities to the workers and in addition cheapening consumption. If that is not possible—that is to say, if the profit from the increased supply at home, together with the profit from the reduced supply abroad, fails to cover total costs including interest—then the industry in question is expanded beyond economically justifiable limits, and it is in the interest of all the productive factors concerned, excepting only the cartel magnates, for capital and labor to move into other industries, something that is necessary and always possible. This constellation of interests is not altered by the circumstance that export monopolism is often able and willing to do things for its workers in the social welfare sphere, thus allowing them to share in its profits.[13] For what makes this possible is, after all, nothing but exploitation of the consumer. If we may speak of the impoverishment of the workers anywhere within the world of capitalism, then a tendency to such impoverishment is apparent here, at least in a relative sense—though actually that tendency has slowed up since the turn of the century. If it is ever true that there is not a trace of parallelism of economic interests between entrepreneurs and workers, but instead only a sharp economic conflict—and usually there is much exaggeration in such statements—then this is true here. Chamberlain had every reason to appeal to national sentiment, to mock the petty calculation of immediate advantage, and to call out to the workers: "Learn to think imperially!" For the English worker knew what he was about, despite the banner headlines on the front pages of the yellow press: "Tariff Reform Means Work For All," and so on.

The fact that the balance sheet of export monopolism is anything but a brilliant success, even for the entrepreneurs, has been glossed over only by an upswing that stemmed from sources other than export monopolism itself. The hope of a future of dominion, to follow the struggles of the present, is but poor solace for the losses in that struggle. Should such a policy become general, the losses—admitted or not—of each individual nation would be even greater, the winnings even smaller. And if the export monopolists have not done too well, the non-monopolist industries of England have hardly suffered from the dumping policies followed by other nations. The British steel industry may have suffered (though it was by no means in serious danger), but in return all the other English industries actually enjoyed, at the expense of the foreign dumpers, a production premium in the form of abnormally low prices for iron and ferrous products. The sugar industry may have been unable to maintain itself in England, but in return sugar-using industries developed in England as they did nowhere else. To those entrepreneurs, moreover, who never succeeded in gaining leading positions in the cartels, the enjoyment of an assured return is often but a poor substitute for lost opportunities for growth. Thus we can understand the fact that even in entrepreneurial circles dissatisfaction with such a policy arose, and while one group entertained the thought of forcible expansion as a last resort, another was led into an attitude of opposition. In all the protectionist countries, therefore, we have had, for the past twenty years, anti-dumping legislation, primarily as an instrument of tariff policy. This legislation, it is true, is directed primarily against foreign dumping rather than against dumping by domestic enterprise, and hence it becomes a new weapon in the hands of the monopoly interests. But it is also true that its political basis lies partly in circles and attitudes opposed on principle to export aggression and for this reason anxious to make such a policy impossible for domestic enterprise. It must be admitted that such opposition often suffers from inappropriate techniques and from the influence of lay catchwords. But given peaceful development, it may be assumed that the opposition would gradually turn directly against dumping by domestic cartels.

This countermovement against export monopolism, within capitalism rather than opposed to it, would mean little if it were merely the political death struggle of a moribund economic order which is giving way to a new phase of development. If the cartel with its policy of export aggression stood face to face with non-cartelized factory industry, as that industry once faced handicraft industry, then even the most vigorous opposition could scarcely change the ultimate outcome or the fundamental significance of the process. But it cannot be emphasized sharply enough that such is not the case. Export monopolism does *not* grow from the inherent laws of capitalist development. The character of capitalism leads to large-scale production, but with few exceptions large-scale production does *not* lead to the kind of unlimited concentration that would leave but one or only a few firms in each industry. On the contrary, any plant runs up against limits to its growth in a given location; and the growth of combinations which would make sense under a system of free trade encounters limits of organizational efficiency. Beyond these limits there is no tendency toward combination inherent in the competitive system. In particular, the rise of trusts and cartels—a phenomenon quite different from the trend to large-scale production with which it is often confused—can never be explained by the automatism of the competitive system. This follows from the very fact that trusts and cartels can attain their primary purpose—to pursue a monopoly policy—only behind protective tariffs, with-

out which they would lose their essential significance. But
protective tariffs do not automatically grow from the competitive system. They are the fruit of political action—*a type
of action that by no means reflects the objective interests of
all those concerned* but that, on the contrary, becomes impossible as soon as the majority of those whose consent is
necessary realize their true interests. To some extent it is obvious, and for the rest it will be presently shown, that the
interests of the minority, quite appropriately expressed in
support of a protective tariff, do not stem from capitalism as
such. It follows that *it is a basic fallacy to describe imperialism as a necessary phase of capitalism, or even to speak of
the development of capitalism into imperialism.* We have
seen before that the mode of life of the capitalist world does
not favor imperialist attitudes. We now see that the alignment of interests in a capitalist economy—even the interests
of its upper strata—by no means points unequivocally in the
direction of imperialism. We now come to the final step in
our line of reasoning.

Since we cannot derive even export monopolism from any
tendencies of the competitive system toward big enterprise,
we must find some other explanation. A glance at the original purpose of tariffs provides what we need. Tariffs sprang
from the financial interests of the monarchy. They were a
method of exploiting the trader which differed from the
method of the robber baron in the same way that the royal
chase differed from the method of the poacher. They were
in line with the royal prerogatives of safe conduct, of protection for the Jews, of the granting of market rights, and so
forth. From the thirteenth century onward this method was
progressively refined in the autocratic state, less and less
emphasis being placed on the direct monetary yield of customs revenues, and more and more on their indirect effect
in creating productive taxable objects. In other words, while
the protective value of a tariff counted, it counted only from
the viewpoint of the ultimate monetary advantage of the
sovereign. It does not matter, for our purposes, that occasionally this policy, under the influence of lay notions of eco-

nomics, blundered badly in the choice of its methods. (From the viewpoint of autocratic interest, incidentally, such measures were not nearly so self-defeating as they were from the viewpoint of the national economy.) Every customs house, every privilege conferring the right to produce, market, or store, thus created a new economic situation which deflected trade and industry into "unnatural" channels. All tariffs, rights, and the like became the seed bed for economic growth that could have neither sprung up nor maintained itself without them. Further, all such economic institutions dictated by autocratic interest were surrounded by manifold interests of people who were dependent on them and now began to demand their continuance—a wholly paradoxical though at the same time quite understandable situation. The trading and manufacturing bourgeoisie was all the more aware of its dependence on the sovereign, since it needed his protection against the remaining feudal powers; and the uncertainties of the times, together with the lack of great consuming centers, impeded the rise of free economic competition. Insofar as commerce and manufacturing came into being at all, therefore, they arose under the sign of monopolistic interest. Thus the bourgeoisie willingly allowed itself to be molded into one of the power instruments of the monarchy, both in a territorial and in a national sense. It is even true that the bourgeoisie, because of the character of its interests and the kind of economic outlook that corresponded to those interests, made an essential contribution to the emergence of modern nationalism. Another factor that worked in the same direction was the financial relation between the great merchant houses and the sovereign. This theory of the nature of the relationship between the autocratic state and the bourgeoisie is not refuted by pointing out that it was precisely the mercantile republics of the Middle Ages and the early modern period that initially pursued a policy of mercantilism. They were no more than enclaves in a world pervaded by the struggle among feudal powers. The Hanseatic League and Venice, for example, could maintain themselves only as military powers. could pursue their business only by means of fortified bases, warehousing privileges, protective treaties. This forced the people to stand shoulder to shoulder, made the exploitation of political gains with a corporate and monopolistic spirit. Wherever autocratic power vanished at an early date—as in the Netherlands and later in England—and the protective interest receded into the background, they swiftly discovered that trade must be free—"free to the nethermost recesses of hell."

Trade and industry of the early capitalist period thus remained strongly pervaded with precapitalist methods, bore the stamp of autocracy, and served its interests, either willingly or by force. With its traditional habits of feeling, thinking, and acting molded along such lines, the bourgeoisie entered the Industrial Revolution. It was shaped, in other words, by the needs and interests of an environment that was essentially non-capitalist, or at least precapitalist—needs stemming not from the nature of the capitalist economy as such but from the fact of the coexistence of early capitalism with another and at first overwhelmingly powerful mode of life and business. Established habits of thought and action tend to persist, and hence the spirit of guild and monopoly at first maintained itself, and was only slowly undermined, even where capitalism was in sole possession of the field. Actually capitalism did not fully prevail *anywhere* on the Continent. Existing economic interests, "artificially" shaped by the autocratic state, remained dependent on the "protection" of the state. The industrial organism, such as it was, would not have been able to withstand free competition. Even where the old barriers crumbled in the autocratic state, the people did not all at once flock to the clear track. They were creatures of mercantilism and even earlier periods, and many of them huddled together and protested against the affront of being forced to depend on their own ability. They cried for paternalism, for protection, for forcible restraint of strangers, and above all for tariffs. They met with partial success, particularly because capitalism failed to take radical action in the agrarian field. Capitalism did bring about many changes on the land, springing in part from its automatic mechanisms, in part from the political trends it engendered —abolition of serfdom, freeing the soil from feudal entanglements, and so on—but initially it did not alter the basic outlines of the social structure of the countryside. Even less did it affect the spirit of the people, and least of all their political goals. This explains why the features and trends of autocracy —including imperialism—proved so resistant, why they exerted such a powerful influence on capitalist development, why the old export monopolism could live on and merge into the new.

These are facts of fundamental significance to an understanding of the soul of modern Europe. Had the ruling class of the Middle Ages—the war-oriented nobility—changed its profession and function and become the ruling class of the capitalist world; or had developing capitalism swept it away, put it out of business, instead of merely clashing head-on with it in the agrarian sphere—then much would have been different in the life of modern peoples. But as things actually were, neither eventuality occurred; or, more correctly, both are taking place, only at a very slow pace. The two groups of landowners remain social classes clearly distinguishable from the groupings of the capitalist world. The social pyramid of the present age has been formed, not by the substance and laws of capitalism alone, but by two different social substances, and by the laws of two different epochs. Whoever seeks to understand Europe must not forget this and concentrate all attention on the indubitably basic truth that one of these substances tends to be absorbed by the other and thus the sharpest of all class conflicts tends to be eliminated. Whoever seeks to understand Europe must not overlook that even today its life, its ideology, its politics are greatly under the influence of the feudal "substance," that while the bourgeoisie can assert its interests everywhere, it "rules" only in exceptional circumstances, and then only briefly. The bourgeois outside his office and the professional man of capitalism outside his profession cut a very sorry figure. Their spiritual leader is the rootless "intellectual," a slender reed open to every impulse and a prey to unrestrained emotionalism. The "feudal" elements, on the other hand, have both feet on the ground, even psychologically speaking. Their ideology is as stable as their mode of life. They believe certain things to be really true, others to be really false. This quality of possessing a definite character and cast of mind as a class, this simplicity and solidity of social and spiritual position extends their power far beyond their actual bases, gives them the ability to assimilate new elements, to make others serve their purposes—in a word, gives them *prestige,* something to which the bourgeois, as is well known, always looks up, something with which he tends to ally himself, despite all actual conflicts.

The nobility entered the modern world in the form into which it had been shaped by the autocratic state—the same state that had also molded the bourgeoisie. It was the sovereign who disciplined the nobility, instilled loyalty into it, "statized" it, and, as we have shown, imperialized it. He turned its nationalist sentiments—as in the case of the bourgeoisie—into an aggressive nationalism, and then made it a pillar of his organization, particularly his war machine. It had not been that in the immediately preceding period. Rising absolutism had at first availed itself of much more dependent organs. For that very reason, in his position as leader of the feudal powers and as warlord, the sovereign survived the onset of the Industrial Revolution, and as a rule—except in France—won victory over political revolution. The bourgeoisie did not simply supplant the sovereign, nor did it make him its leader, as did the nobility. It merely wrested a portion of his power from him and for the rest submitted to him. It did not take over from the sovereign the state as an abstract form of organization. The state remained a special social power, confronting the bourgeoise. In some countries it has continued to play that role to the present day. It is in the *state* that the bourgeoisie with its interests seeks refuge, protection against external and even domestic enemies. The bourgeoisie seeks to win over the state for itself, and in return serves the state and state interests that are different from its own. Imbued with the spirit of the old autocracy, trained by it, the bourgeoisie often takes over its ideology, even where, as in France, the sovereign is eliminated and the official power of the nobility has been broken. Because the sovereign needed soldiers, the modern bourgeois—at least in his slogans—is an even more vehement advocate of an increasing population. Because the sovereign was in a position to exploit conquests, needed them to be a victorious warlord, the bourgeoisie thirsts for national glory—even in France, worshiping a headless body, as it were. Because the sovereign found a large gold hoard useful, the bourgeoisie even today cannot be swerved from its bullionist prejudices. Because the autocratic state paid attention to the trader and manufacturer chiefly as the most important sources of taxes and credits, today even the intellectual who has not a shred of property looks on international commerce, not from the viewpoint of the consumer, but from that of the trader and exporter. Because pugnacious sovereigns stood in constant fear of attack by their equally pugnacious neighbors, the modern bourgeois attributes aggressive designs to neighboring peoples. All such modes of thought are essentially non-capitalist. Indeed, they vanish most quickly wherever capitalism fully prevails. They are survivals of the autocratic alignment of interests, and they endure wherever the autocratic state endures on the old basis and with the old orientation, even though more and more democratized and otherwise transformed. They bear witness to the extent to which essentially imperialist absolutism has patterned not only the economy of the bourgeoisie but also its mind—in the interests of autocracy and against those of the bourgeoisie itself.

This significant dichotomy in the bourgeois mind—which in part explains its wretched weakness in politics, culture, and life generally; earns it the understandable contempt of the Left and the Right; and proves the accuracy of our diagnosis—is best exemplified by two phenomena that are very close to our subject: present-day nationalism and militarism. Nationalism is affirmative awareness of national character, together with an aggressive sense of superiority. It arose from the autocratic state. In conservatives, nationalism in general is understandable as an inherited orientation, as a mutation of the battle instincts of the medieval knights, and finally as a political stalking horse on the domestic scene; and conservatives are fond of reproaching the bourgeois with a lack of nationalism, which from their point of view, is evaluated in a positive sense. Socialists, on the other hand, equally understandably exclude nationalism from their general ideology, because of the essential interests of the proletariat, and by virtue of their domestic opposition to the conservative stalking horse; they, in turn, not only reproach the bourgeoisie with an excess of nationalism (which they, of course, evaluate in a negative sense) but actually identify nationalism and even the very idea of the nation with bourgeois ideology. The curious thing is that both of these groups are right in their criticism of the bourgeoisie. For, as we have seen, the mode of life that flows logically from the nature of capitalism necessarily implies an anti-nationalist orientation in politics and culture. This orientation actually prevails. We find a great many anti-nationalist members of the middle class, and even more who merely parrot the catchwords of nationalism. In the capitalist world it is actually not big business and industry at all that are the carriers of nationalist trends, but the intellectual, and the content of *his* ideology is explained not so much from definite class interests as from chance emotion and individual interest. But the submission of the bourgeoisie to the powers of autocracy, its alliance with them, its economic and psychological patterning by them—all these tend to push the bourgeois in a nationalist direction; and this too we find prevalent, especially among the chief exponents of export monopolism. The relationship between the bourgeoisie and militarism is quite similar. Militarism is not necessarily a foregone conclusion when a nation maintains a large army, but only when high military circles become a political power. The criterion is whether leading generals as such wield political influence and whether the responsible statesmen can act only with their consent. That is possible only when the officer corps is linked to a definite social class, as in Japan, and can assimilate to its position individuals who do not belong to it by birth. Militarism too is rooted in the autocratic state. And again the same reproaches are made against the bourgeois from both sides—quite properly too. According to the "pure" capitalist mode of life, the bourgeois is unwarlike. The alignment of capitalist interests should make him utterly reject military methods, put him in opposition to the professional soldier. Significantly, we see this in the example of England where, first, the struggle against a standing army generally and, next, opposition to its elaboration, furnished bourgeois politicians with their most popular slogan: "retrenchment." Even naval appropriations have encountered resistance. We find similar trends in other countries, though they are less strongly developed. The continental bourgeois, however, was used to the sight of troops. He regarded an army almost as a necessary component of the social order, ever since it had been his terrible taskmaster in the Thirty Years' War. He had no power at all to abolish the army. He might have done so if he had had the power; but not having it, he considered the fact that the army might be useful to him. In his "artificial" economic situation and because of his submission to the sovereign, he thus grew disposed toward militarism, especially where export monopolism flourished. The intellectuals, many of whom still maintained special relationships with feudal elements, were so disposed to an even greater degree.[14]

Just as we once found a dichotomy in the social pyramid, so now we find everywhere, in every aspect of the bourgeois portion of the modern world, a dichotomy of attitudes and interests. Our examples also show in what way the two components work together. Nationalism and militarism, while not creatures of capitalism, become "capitalized" and in the end draw their best energies from capitalism. Capitalism involves them in its workings and thereby keeps them alive, politically as well as economically. And they, in turn, affect capitalism, cause it to deviate from the course it might have followed alone, support many of its interests.

Here we find that we have penetrated to the historical as

well as the sociological sources of modern imperialism. It does not *coincide* with nationalism and militarism, though it *fuses* with them by supporting them as it is supported by them. It too is—not only historically, but also sociologically —a heritage of the autocratic state, of its structural elements, organizational forms, interest alignments, and human attitudes, the outcome of precapitalist forces which the autocratic state has reorganized, in part by the methods of early capitalism. It would never have been evolved by the "inner logic" of capitalism itself. This is true even of mere export monopolism. It too has its sources in absolutist policy and the action habits of an essentially precapitalist environment. That it was able to develop to its present dimensions is owing to the momentum of a situation once created, which continued to engender ever new "artificial" economic structures, that is, those which maintain themselves by political power alone. In most of the countries addicted to export monopolism it is also owing to the fact that the old autocratic state and the old attitude of the bourgeoisie toward it were so vigorously maintained. But export monopolism, to go a step further, is not yet imperialism. And even if it had been able to arise without protective tariffs, it would never have developed into imperialism in the hands of an unwarlike bourgeoisie. If this did happen, it was only because the heritage included the war machine, together with its sociopsychological aura and aggressive bent, and because a class oriented toward war maintained itself in a ruling position. This class clung to its domestic interest in war, and the promilitary interests among the bourgeoisie were able to ally themselves with it. This alliance kept alive war instincts and ideas of overlordship, male supremacy, and triumphant glory —ideas that would have otherwise long since died. It led to social conditions that, while they ultimately stem from the conditions of production, cannot be explained from capitalist production methods alone. And it often impresses its mark on present-day politics, threatening Europe with the constant danger of war.

This diagnosis also bears the prognosis of imperialism.

The precapitalist elements in our social life may still have great vitality; special circumstances in national life may revive them from time to time; but in the end the climate of the modern world must destroy them. This is all the more certain since their props in the modern capitalist world are not of the most durable material. Whatever opinion is held concerning the vitality of capitalism itself, whatever the life span predicted for it, it is bound to withstand the onslaughts of its enemies and its own irrationality much longer than essentially untenable export monopolism—untenable even from the capitalist point of view. Export monopolism may perish in revolution, or it may be peacefully relinquished; this may happen soon, or it may take some time and require desperate struggle; but one thing is certain—it *will* happen. This will immediately dispose of neither warlike instincts nor structural elements and organizational forms oriented toward war—and it is to their dispositions and domestic interests that, in my opinion, much more weight must be given in every concrete case of imperialism than to export monopolist interests, which furnish the financial "outpost skirmishes"—a most appropriate term—in many wars. But such factors will be politically overcome in time, no matter what they do to maintain among the people a sense of constant danger of war, with the war machine forever primed for action. And with them, imperialisms will wither and die.

It is not within the scope of this study to offer an ethical, esthetic, cultural, or political evaluation of this process. Whether it heals sores or extinguishes suns is a matter of utter indifference from the viewpoint of this study. It is not the concern of science to judge that. The only point at issue here was to demonstrate, by means of an important example, the ancient truth that the dead always rule the living.

Social Classes in an Ethnically
Homogeneous Environment

PREFATORY NOTE

The basic idea here briefly set forth dates back to the year 1910 and was first presented in a lecture course for laymen on the subject of "State and Society" which I delivered at the University of Czernowitz (Cernauti) in the winter of 1910-1911. Subsequently, at Columbia University in the winter of 1913-1914, I presented it at length in a course entitled "The Theory of Social Classes." Since that time I have never altogether stopped developing my thoughts and analyzing the material on the subject, but after 1916 the topic took second place to other interests. Hence I am glad to seize upon the occasion of a lecture, delivered on November 19, 1926, at the University of Heidelberg, under the title "Leadership and Class Formation," to formulate once again and to publish for the first time a line of reasoning which, according to my present plan of work, I shall be able to work out fully only years from now, if at all. I offer this by way of explanation, though not of excuse, for the gaps and unevennesses in the following presentation, which stand in regrettable contrast to the length of time during which the thoughts matured and the amount of effort that went into them.

The qualifying phrase, "in an ethnically homogeneous environment," is not meant to deny the significance of racial differences in explaining concrete class formations. On the contrary, my early thinking on the subject followed the paths of the racial theory of classes, as it is found in the works of Gumplowicz, upon which I came while I was still at school. One of the strongest impressions of my apprenticeship came from Haddon, the ethnologist, who, in a course given at the London School of Economics late in 1906, demonstrated to us the differing racial types of various classes of Asiatic peoples, with the aid of countless photographs. Nevertheless, this is not the heart of the matter, not the reason why there are social classes. True, even the cursory outline, imperfect in every respect, which I present in the following, must at one point take account of this factor—since no explicit presentation would be possible otherwise. But in order not to complicate the basic features of the picture, I thought it best to exclude the racial factor in what I have to say. When it comes to investigating the "essential nature" of a social phenomenon, it is often proper and necessary to ignore certain external factors that may be quite characteristic or at least common. They may be "essential" in many respects, but not for the purposes in hand.

The theory of social classes has not attracted an amount of study truly commensurate with its fundamental importance. Marx, for example, who recognized its importance and even exaggerated it in one direction, offered a theory of the evolution of classes, but not really a theory of classes themselves. Even so, it is scarcely fair for Sombart to say (*Sozialismus und Soziale Bewegung,* p. 2) that in the works of Guizot, Mignet, and Louis Blanc we "can read everything that can be stated to this day about the nature and growth of social classes." Sombart's own definition (*loc. cit.,* p. 1) offers more than that and deserves to be recognized here as a contribution to the subject. And the widely known theories of the past fifty years do more than merely echo the thoughts of the aforementioned authors (and of Ferguson as well), nor are they made of thin air. Our own views rest, in more or less important points, on the work of Schmoller, which includes much more than merely the element of the division of labor; and on Durkheim and Spann (note the latter's reduction of "class" to "estate," in the *Handwörterbuch der Staatswissenschaften* article, "Klasse und Stand"). In many respects, furthermore, we hark back to Simmel, A. Bauer (*Les Classes sociales,* 1902), and Overberg ("La Classe sociale," *Extrait des Annales de la Société belge de Sociologie,* 1905); as well as to the theory of Bücher, so wittily expressed in the well-known simile about the *mariage de convenance* between occupation and property—though it is a theory that never goes much beneath the surface or past the foreground. The book by P. E. Fahlbeck, excellent in many individual sections, seems to us to be merely skirting the problem, which appears often enough. As for the book by Niceforo, it represents no more than a first step along a promising avenue of approach and hence, understandably, succeeds only in part. We are compelled to forego debating the views of all these authors, to whom we should have to add the majority of sociologists and "historians of society" (such as Riehl and Rossbach), though such a method of presentation might best serve to set forth our own concepts in detail and to buttress them against objections.

Our subject owes much more to legal and social history; to ethnology (where, unfortunately, the wrong questions are often asked and there is lack of a real grasp of the problem); to the study of the family; and to eugenics—for those, that is, who know how to recognize the relevance of what these disciplines have to offer. Beyond all this, the subject— and this is what constitutes its fascination—poses a wealth of new questions, offers outlooks on untilled fields, foreshadows sciences of the future. Roaming it, one often has a strange feeling, as though the social sciences of today, almost on purpose, were dealing with relative side-issues; as though some day—and perhaps soon—the things we now believe will be discounted. But this is not an aspect that I wish to bring to the fore. Quite the contrary. My purpose is to present, not only as briefly but as soberly as possible, a sharply delimited series of problems, together with their corresponding solutions. The wider vistas must open up to the reader spontaneously or not at all.

THE PROBLEM OF CLASSES

1. We here mean by classes those social phenomena with which we are all familiar—social entities which we observe but which are not of our making. In this sense every social class is a special social organism, living, acting, and suffering as such and in need of being understood as such.[1] Yet the concept of class occurs in the social sciences in still another meaning—a meaning shared with many other sciences. In this sense it still corresponds to a set of facts, but not to any specific phenomenon of reality. Here it becomes a matter of classifying different things according to certain chosen characteristics. Viewed in this sense, class is a creation of the researcher, owes its existence to his organizing touch. These two meanings are often annoyingly mixed up in our social-science thinking, and we therefore emphasize what should be self-evident, namely, that there is not the slightest connection between them as a matter of necessity. Whenever there is any actual coincidence of their contents, this is either a matter of chance, or—if it is really more than that—must be demonstrated, generally or specifically, by means of pertinent rules of evidence. It can never be assumed as a matter of course. This word of caution applies especially to the field

in which theoretical economics operates. In theoretical economics, a landlord—the very term implies the confusion we oppose—is anyone who is in possession of the services of land. But not only do such people not form a social class. They are divided by one of the most conspicuous class cleavages of all. And the working class, in the sense of economic theory, includes the prosperous lawyer as well as the ditchdigger. These classes are classes only in the sense that they result from the scholar's classification of economic subjects. Yet they are often thought and spoken of as though they *were* classes in the sense of the social phenomenon we here seek to investigate. The two reasons that explain this situation actually make it more troublesome than it would otherwise be. There is, first, the fact that the characteristic by which the economist classifies does have some connection with the real phenomenon. Then there is the fact that the economic theorist finds it exceedingly difficult to confine himself strictly to his problems, to resist the temptation to enliven his presentation with something that fascinates most of his readers—in other words, to stoke his sputtering engine with the potent fuel of the class struggle. Hence the amusing circumstance that some people view any distinction between economic theory and the facts of social class as evidence of the most abysmal failure to grasp the point at issue; while others see any fusion of the two as the most abysmal analytical blundering. Hence, too, the fact that the very term class struggle, let alone the idea behind it, has fallen into discredit among the best minds in science and politics alike— in much the same way that the overpowering impression of the Palazzo Strozzi loses so much by its inescapable juxtaposition with the frightful pseudo-architecture of modern apartment houses.

2. Of the many sociological problems which beset the field of class theory—the scientific rather than the philosophical theory, the sociological rather than the immediately economic—four emerge distinctly. First, there is the problem of the *nature* of class (which is perhaps, and even probably, different for each individual scientific discipline, and for each

purpose pursued within such a discipline)—and, as part of this problem, the function of class in the vital processes of the social whole. Fundamentally different, at least theoretically, is the problem of class *cohesion*—the factors that make of every social class, as we put it, a special living social organism, that prevent the group from scattering like a heap of billiard balls. Again fundamentally distinct is the problem of class *formation*—the question of why the social whole, as far as our eye can reach, has never been homogeneous, always revealing this particular, obviously organic stratification. Finally, we must realize—and we shall presently revert to this point—that this problem is again wholly different from the series of problems that are concerned with the *concrete causes and conditions* of an individually determined, historically given class structure—a distinction that is analogous to that between the problem of the theory of prices in general and problems such as the explanation of the level of milk prices in the year 1919.

We are not, at this point, seeking a definition that would anticipate the solution of our problem. What we need, rather, is a characteristic that will enable us, in each case, to recognize a social class and to distinguish it from other social classes—a characteristic that will show on the surface and, if possible, on the surface alone; that will be as clear or as fuzzy as the situation itself is at first glance. Class is something more than an aggregation of class members. It is something else, and this something cannot be recognized in the behavior of the individual class member. A class is aware of its identity as a whole, sublimates itself as such, has its own peculiar life and characteristic "spirit." Yet one essential peculiarity—possibly a consequence, possibly an intermediate cause—of the class phenomenon lies in the fact that class members behave toward one another in a fashion characteristically different from their conduct toward members of other classes. They are in closer association with one another; they understand one another better; they work more readily in concert; they close ranks and erect barriers against the outside; they look out into the same segment of the world, with the same eyes, from the same viewpoint, in the same direction. These are familiar observations, and among explanations which are traditionally adduced are the similarity of the class situation and the basic class type.

To this extent the behavior of people toward one another is a very dependable and useful *symptom* of the presence or absence of class cohesion among them—although it does not, of course, go very deeply, let alone constitute a cause. Even more on the surface—a symptom of a symptom, so to speak, though it hints at a far-reaching basic orientation—is the specific way in which people engage in social intercourse. These ways are decisively influenced by the degree of "shared social *a priori*," as we might say with Simmel. Social intercourse within class barriers is promoted by the similarity of manners and habits of life, of things that are evaluated in a positive or negative sense, that arouse interest. In intercourse across class borders, differences on all these points repel and inhibit sympathy. There are always a number of delicate matters that must be avoided, things that seem strange and even absurd to the other class. The participants in social intercourse between different classes are always on their best behavior, so to speak, making their conduct forced and unnatural. The difference between intercourse within the class and outside the class is the same as the difference between swimming with and against the tide. The most important symptom of this situation is the ease or difficulty with which members of different classes contract legally and socially recognized marriages. Hence we find a suitable definition of the class—one that makes it outwardly recognizable and involves no class theory—in the fact that intermarriage prevails among its members, socially rather than legally.[2] This criterion is especially useful for our purposes, because we limit our study to the class phenomenon in a racially homogeneous environment, thus eliminating the most important additional impediment to intermarriage.[3]

3. Our study applies to the third of the four questions we have distinguished—to the others only to the extent that it is unavoidable. Let us begin by briefly discussing three diffi-

culties in our way—a consideration of each of them already constituting an objective step toward our goal.

First: We seek to interpret the class phenomenon in the same sense in which we understand social phenomena generally, that is, as *adaptations* to existing needs, grasped by the observer—ourselves—as such. We shall pass over the logical difficulties inherent in even this simple statement, such as whether it is admissible to apply our own conceptual modes to cultures remote from us. There is also the question of the extent to which the condition of culturally primitive peoples in our own time may be taken as a clue to the past state of modern civilized peoples, and the even more important question of the extent to which historical data are at all valid for theoretical purposes. One difficulty, however, we must face. Unless specifically proven, it is an erroneous assumption that social phenomena to which the same name has been applied over thousands of years are always the same things, merely in different form. This is best seen in the history of social institutions. Anyone will realize that common ownership of land in the ancient Germanic village community—supposing, for the moment, that its existence had been proven—is something altogether different from common land ownership in present-day Germany. Yet the term ownership is used as though it always implied the same basic concept. Obviously this can be true only in a very special sense, to be carefully delimited in each case. When taken for granted, it becomes a source of one-sided and invalid constructions. The fact that there may occur in the language of law and life of a given period expressions that we regard as equivalent to our chosen concept, proves nothing, even when those expressions were actually used in an equivalent sense. Similarly, the actuality of the institution we call marriage has changed so greatly in the course of time that it is quite inadmissible to regard that institution always as the same phenomenon, from a general sociological viewpoint and without reference to a specific research purpose. This does not mean that we renounce the habit, indispensable in analysis, of seeking, wherever possible, the same essential character in the most diverse forms. But the existence of that character must be a fact, its establishment the result of study, not a mere postulate. This applies to our problem as well. When we speak of "the" class phenomenon and take it to mean that group differences in social values, found everywhere, though under varying conditions, are everywhere explained by the same theory, that is not even a working hypothesis, but merely a method of presentation in which the result is anticipated—a result that has meaning only from the viewpoint of the particular theory in question. "Master classes," for example, do not exist everywhere —if, indeed, the concept of "master" has a precise content at all.

Second: The class membership of an individual is a primary fact, originally quite independent of his will. But he does not always confirm that allegiance by his conduct. As is well known, it is common for nonmembers of a class to work with and on behalf of that class, especially in a political sense, while members of a class may actually work against it. Such cases are familiar from everyday life—they are called fellow travelers, renegades, and the like. This phenomenon must be distinguished, on the one hand, from a situation in which an entire class, or at least its leadership, behaves differently from what might be expected from its class orientation; and, on the other hand, from a situation in which the individual, by virtue of his own functional position, comes into conflict with his class. There is room for differences of opinion on these points. For example, one may see in them aberrations from the normal pattern that hold no particular interest, that have no special significance to an understanding of society, that are often exceptions to the rule more apparent than real. Those who view the class struggle as the core of all historical explanation will generally incline to such opinions and seek to explain away conflicting evidence. From another viewpoint, however, these phenomena become the key to an understanding of political history—one without which its actual course and in particular its class evolution become altogether incomprehensible. To whatever class theory one may adhere, there is always the necessity of choosing between these viewpoints. The phenomena alluded to, of course, complicate not only the realities of social life but also its intellectual perception. We think that our line of reasoning will fully answer this question, and we shall not revert to it.

Third: Every social situation is the heritage of preceding situations and takes over from them not only their cultures, their dispositions, and their "spirit," but also elements of their social structure and concentrations of power. This fact is of itself interesting. The social pyramid is never made of a single substance, is never seamless. There is no single *Zeitgeist*, except in the sense of a construct. This means that in explaining any historical course or situation, account must be taken of the fact that much in it can be explained only by the survival of elements that are actually alien to its own trends. This is, of course self-evident, but it does become a source of practical difficulties and diagnostic problems. Another implication is that the coexistence of essentially different mentalities and objective sets of facts must form part of any general theory. Thus the economic interpretation of history, for example, would at once become untenable and unrealistic—indeed, some easily demolished objections to it are explained from this fact—if its formulation failed to consider that the manner in which production methods shape social life is essentially influenced by the fact that the human protagonists have always been shaped by past situations. When applied to our problem, this means, first, that any theory of class structure, in dealing with a given historical period, must include prior class structures among its data; and then, that any general theory of classes and class formation must explain the fact that classes coexisting at any given time bear the marks of different centuries on their brow, so to speak—that they stem from varying conditions. This is in the essential nature of the matter, an aspect of the nature of the class phenomenon.

Classes, once they have come into being, harden in their mold and perpetuate themselves, even when the social conditions that created them have disappeared.

In this connection it becomes apparent that in the field of our own problem this difficulty bears an aspect lacking in many other problems. When one seeks to render modern banking comprehensible, for example, one can trace its historical origins, since doubtless there were economic situations in which there was no banking, and others in which the beginnings of banking can be observed. But this is impossible in the case of class, for there are no amorphous societies in this sense—societies, that is, in which the absence of our phenomenon can be demonstrated beyond doubt. Its presence may be more or less strongly marked, a distinction of great importance for our solution of the class problem. But neither historically nor ethnologically has its utter absence been demonstrated in even a single case, although there has been no dearth either of attempts in that direction (in eighteenth-century theories of culture) or of an inclination to assume the existence of classless situations.[4] We must therefore forego any aid from this side, whatever it may be worth,[5] though the ethnological material nevertheless retains fundamental significance for us. If we wanted to start from a classless society, the only cases we could draw upon would be those in which societies are formed accidentally, in which whatever class orientations the participants may have either count for nothing or lack the time to assert themselves—cases, in other words, like that of a ship in danger, a burning theater, and so on. We do not completely discount the value of such cases, but quite apparently we cannot do very much with them. Any study of classes and class situations therefore leads, in unending regression, to other classes and class situations, just as any explanation of the circular flow of the economic process always leads back, without any logical stopping point, to the preceding circular flow that furnishes the data for the one to follow. Similarly—though less closely so—analysis of the economic value of goods always leads back from a use value to a cost value and back again to a use value, so that it seems to turn in a circle. Yet this very analogy points to the logical way out. The general and mutual interdependence of values and prices in an economic situation does not prevent us from finding an all-encompassing explanatory principle; and the fact of regression in our own case does not mean the non-existence of a principle that will explain the formation, nature, and basic laws of classes—though this fact naturally does not necessarily furnish us with such a principle. If we cannot derive the sought-for principle from the genesis of classes in a classless state, it may yet emerge from a study of how classes function and what happens to them, especially from actual observation of the changes in the relationship of existing classes to one another and of individuals within the class structure—*provided* it can be shown that the elements explaining such changes also include the reason why classes exist at all.

THE RISE AND FALL OF FAMILIES WITHIN A CLASS

4. We have said that allegiance to a certain class is a foreordained fact for the individual—that he is *born* into a given class situation. This is an objective situation, quite independent of what the individual does or wants to do, indeed limiting the scope of his behavior to a characteristic pattern. The individual belongs to a given class neither by choice, nor by any other action, nor by innate qualities—in sum, his class membership is not individual at all. It stems from his membership in a given clan or lineage. The family, not the physical person, is the true unit of class and class theory.[1]

We shall for the moment postulate given class situations, as though every social class that ever existed were made up simply of a certain number of family units, which, for some reason or other, had chanced into their class and had persisted in it, forbidding other people access to it—in other words, as though class barriers were insurmountable. Now it is beyond dispute that within a class the relative position of families is forever shifting, that some families rise within their class, while others fall. And we are interested in the reasons *why* this happens. This can best be studied in individual historical situations. The scope of our own study imposes certain limitations on us, and we therefore choose but two examples that demonstrate the points in question —the German aristocracy of the Hohenstaufen period, and the industrial bourgeoisie of capitalism at its prime. It will be seen at once that the arguments to be enumerated apply beyond the cases under consideration.

One reason for the rise or fall of a family manifestly applies so generally that it can be discussed without reference to a specific example. This is chance. We take this to mean the occurrence of favorable or unfavorable events that are independent of the behavior of the family in question, or of its position.[2] Only in rare instances is an event of this nature significant enough to exert a critical and enduring effect on the fate of a family, in a way that might not have happened otherwise. Even rarer are those cases in which not only the occurrence but also the effect of the event on the family's position is independent of its behavior—for even where chance operates, its effects are usually exploited or overcome. An example might be the gain in wealth and position accruing to the few aristocratic families who happened to own the land on which present-day London is built. The position of the Grosvenors (Westminster), for example, rests wholly on this chance, while that of the Russells (Bedford) and Howards (Norfolk) was greatly enhanced thereby. The significance of such accidents in the total picture of family history is too slight to figure as more than an aberration, important only to an understanding of individual cases or groups of cases. We can also assess as quite insignificant the number of cases in which a series of unre-

lated chances, each one alone unimportant, but the sum total carrying great weight, lifts up a family or depresses it.
For, by the law of probability, such events are bound to can-
cel each other out. Of course, this does not necessarily happen in the individual case. But no valid theory to account
for the constant shifting of family positions can be built on
such a foundation.

5. The German nobility of the Hohenstaufen period
formed not one class, but two: first, the princes (small in
number after the Hohenstaufen reforms) and princely
lieges [*fürstengenossen*] (who numbered in the hundreds,
though most families of that position in the thirteenth century were extinct by the fifteenth); and second, the mere
knights [*ritterliche Burgherren*]. There were differences between these two classes, not only in rank but also in law,
mode of life, and power; nor did they intermarry. It was in
the upper of the two that the restratification took place
which found expression in the so-called constitutional reform of the Hohenstaufen period; but in both classes certain
families, in terms of wealth and prestige, rose high above
the level at which we find them at the outset of the period;
while others sank down, languished, and grew impoverished. Why?

In the first place, there is an automatic increment to a position once elevated. To the family that looms above its fellows accrue new vassals, tenants, and properties, which slip
from the grasp of families in decline. The rising family has
better chances and is able to exploit them more effectively
than the family on the downgrade. Rising power always in-
vests in new power. But the explanatory value of this factor is greatly limited by the fact that it already presupposes
an elevated or rising position. Of itself it would evidently
account for only a modest increment, beyond which further
gains would be dependent on new successes—as demonstrated by the rapid disintegration of even high positions.
It can therefore be considered only a consequence and intermediate cause.

In the second place, hard-headed and practical shrewdness in the management of a given position plays a very great part. This factor manifestly explains a great deal about differences in family destiny, more specifically in three directions. Above all, the rise of many families is explained almost completely, that of others in part, by a single-minded marriage policy pursued over centuries with the object of enhancing their positions. Next, the success of such a policy, and of course success in general, requires an economic mobility that in turn presupposes shrewd and often ruthless exploitation of existing sources of revenue and rational utilization of their yield. Finally, the management of family position within the feudal system—and this means above all the energetic repression of neighboring lords, and sometimes also of vassals—presents a crucial and difficult problem which is solved with varying degrees of success. In certain outstanding cases, positions at the top are gained in this way rather than by the prior granting of privileges and rights on the part of the king—something that comes only subsequently. In other cases, the decline of a house can be explained by its failure to manage its position properly in spite of the fact that its claim to princely rank is as good as, or even better than, those that make the grade. This, in particular, explains a good deal about the varying success of princes—and, we may say in passing, about the uneven growth of territories in later ages.

In the third place, shifts in family position follow from differences in the way in which families stand up in the service of their feudal superiors. With some variations, this, of course, means almost exclusively war service. Only among the lower ranks of the knights does administrative and diplomatic skill count. High Church office is very important as a means of elevating the family—in Italy, for example, though not so much in Germany—at the time we are considering. Outstanding examples of such shifts, based on service, are obvious.

In the fourth place, success in wars undertaken on their own account elevates many families, while failure submerges others. This is quite evident at the highest levels. But even the lowliest knight, whose resources might be sufficient for only insignificant feuds and depredations, could rise in this fashion, especially if he refrained from going beyond the point at which his environment would join in league against him. Lack of restraint could ruin even families that had risen to the level, for example, of the Kuenringens in Austria below the Enns.[3]

All this is best observed in the rise and further development of the later sovereign territories. The factors which have been enumerated explain even their original size, and certainly fully account for their subsequent expansion or contraction. The fortunes of dynasties rose and fell in keeping with the success or failure of their policies. At bottom, this is really beyond argument. Who, for example, would care to dispute that even in the seventeenth century, Saxony's objective chances for hegemony were incomparably better that those of Brandenburg? Yet step by step Saxony lost its position, by persistently poor management on every hand, by ill-starred undertakings, by backing the wrong horse—in short by conduct that meant failure, or, to come right out and say so, through incompetence. Brandenburg, on the other hand, rose steadily, by conduct of the opposite kind. Yet apparent as the truth of this matter is, it can easily lead to an overestimate of the autonomy and importance of the physical individual. Nothing is more foreign in us than such an overestimate, let alone an orientation in the manner of Carlyle. We do not for a moment deny the dominance of objective social circumstances. Only the disposition of the people in general, of the stratum and of the individual family, is a part of these circumstances; and once the rest of the environment is given, this element does play the crucial role we claim for it—whether or not it be traced to other elements, which is the great question of the future, but does not here concern us.

6. In the case of the capitalist bourgeoisie of Europe—say, of the post-Napoleonic period—we also hold to the assumption that we are dealing with established data insofar as the situations of the class and of the individual families

are concerned. We presume that each family already owns its enterprise, or its share in one. The only question we ask is this: how does it happen that one family rises, while the other falls—quite apart from accidents, to which we attribute a certain importance but not the crucial role? The rising and falling are facts. No matter which area we study, we always find that the relative position of families in the class situation we have described—other families are of no concern to us at this point—undergoes change, not in such a way that the "big" ones grow bigger and the "small" ones smaller, but typically the other way round. In the textile area of Brno, the silk region of Krefeld, the iron-working district around Birmingham, for example, certain families have maintained their position for more than half a century, in many cases considerably longer. Yet, by and large, the families that led around the middle of the nineteenth century are not on top of the heap today. Some of those that are most successful now were then scarcely recognized as members of the class, while some of those that were most successful then are accepted only with reservations today. Manifestly, concentration and the formation of corporations complicate our analysis, and it will be well if we make a distinction between the competitive private and one-man firm, on the one hand, and the modern large-scale enterprise and trust, on the other.

The characteristic feature of the former is the element of family property and the coincidence of family and business success. A first reason for shifting family position is offered by the automatism of accumulation, asserted by Marx. The "capitalist" who is bigger at the outset of the period captures more profit than the smaller one. His proportionate accumulation is therefore larger, and he improves his productive plant more rapidly. The discrepancy grows, until the wealthier exploiter outstrips the poorer one in the competitive field and forces him to the wall. This view is a typical example of how bias in favor of a theory blinds the theorist to the simplest facts, grotesquely distorting their proportions. Manifestly, the captured surplus value *does not invest itself* but must *be invested*. This means on the one hand that it must not be consumed by the capitalist, and on the other hand that the important point is *how* it is invested. Both factors lead away from the idea of objective automatism to the field of behavior and motive—in other words, from the *social* "force" to the *individual*—physical or family; from the *objective* to the *subjective*. It may be objected that the logic of the social situation forces the individual to invest his profits, that individual motivation is only a fleeting intermediate phase. This is true, as far as it goes, and must be acknowledged by any reasonable person. Naturally the individual psyche is no more than a product, an offshoot, a reflex, and a conductor of the inner necessities of any given situation. But the crucial factor is that the social logic or objective situation does not unequivocally determine *how much* profit shall be invested, and *how* it shall be invested, *unless individual disposition is taken into account*. Yet when that is done, the logic is no longer inherent solely in the system as distinct from the individuality of the industrialist himself. Marx, in fact, in this case as in general, implies an assumption about average behavior—an assumption that includes an economic psychology, however imperfect. The automatism as such does not exist, even though we shall presently encounter its elements—saving and the improvement of productive plant—as elements of industrial-family behavior. We can speak of an automatism, with respect to an existing class position, only in the sense that, as in the earlier example, that position does have a tendency to rise on its own, to a moderate extent, and even more a tendency to maintain itself, because the well-established firm can make better deals, attract new customers and suppliers, and so on.

There is, on the other hand, the very important fact of automatic decline. This occurs invariably when a family behaves according to Marx's description—when it persists in "plowing back into the business" a set proportion of profits, without blazing new trails, without being devoted, heart and soul, to the business alone. In that event it is bound to go under in time, though often only very slowly if the business is on a solid foundation and the mode of life frugal. A steady decline and loss of ground are first observed—what is called "being crowded out of business." This decline *is* automatic, for it is not a matter of omission or commission, but flows instead from the self-actuating logic of the competitive system, by the simple fact of profits running dry. As to the question why this is so, it is answered by the theory of entrepreneurial profit.[4] It seems to me, however, that everybody knows the type of old respectable firm, growing obsolete, despite its integrity, and slowly and inevitably sinking into limbo.

The second reason for the phenomenon with which we are concerned at the moment lies in the disposition to save, which varies from family to family. (If the term "saving" must be avoided as implying a positive value judgment, we can speak of an energetic policy of withholding.) This serves to make the class position secure, and adherence to such a policy over several generations is the factor that in many cases turns small family enterprises into large ones. It is a policy that is very conspicuous in families that practice it. Most of us have observed members of successful business families who watch with extreme care over expenditures which members of other classes, even when their incomes are incomparably smaller, do not hesitate a moment to make. In their personal lives, such families often live with curious frugality, sometimes against a background that, for reasons of prestige, may be quite luxurious and out of keeping with their parsimony. True, of itself this does not carry much weight, though contrary behavior may be one of the most important reasons for a decline.

The third reason lies in differences in efficiency—the quality of technical, commercial, and administrative leadership of the enterprise, primarily along traditional lines. Behavior giving rise to such differences may, for our purposes, be adequately described in terms of hard-headedness, concentration on profit, authority, capacity for work, and inexorable self-discipline, especially in renouncing other aspects of life. This latter feature often escapes consideration, because the outsider is likely to observe these people in the practice of compensatory and conspicuous excesses. The significance of such efficiency lies not so much in immediate results as in increased credit ratings that open up opportunities for expansion.

Actually, among the obstacles in the way of the rise of an industrial family, eventual lack of capital is the least. If it is otherwise in good condition, the family will find that in normal times capital is virtually thrust upon it. Indeed, one may say, with Marshall, that the size of an enterprise—and here that means the position of the family—tends to adapt itself to the ability of the entrepreneur. If he exceeds his personal limitations, resultant failure will trim the size of his enterprise; if he lacks the capital to exploit such personal resources as he does possess, he is likely to find the necessary credit. But in considering this process of expansion, we come upon a fourth reason for the varying success of business dynasties. Such expansion is not simply a matter of saving and efficient routine work. What it implies is precisely departure from routine. Elaboration of an established plant, the introduction of new production methods, the opening up of new markets—indeed, the successful carrying through of new business combinations in general—all these imply risk, trial and error, the overcoming of resistance, factors lacking in the treadmill of routine. Most members of the class are handicapped in this respect. They can follow suit only when someone else has already demonstrated success in practice. Such success requires a capacity for making decisions and the vision to evaluate forcefully the elements in a given situation that are relevant to the achievement of success, while ignoring all others. The rarity of such qualifications explains why competition does not function immediately even when there are no outward barriers, such as cartels; and this circumstance, in turn, explains the size of the profits that often eventuate from such success. This is the typical pattern by which industrial fortunes were made in the nineteenth century, and by which they are made even today; and these factors typically enhance family position, both absolutely and relatively. Neither saving nor efficient management as such are the crucial factors; what is crucial is the successful accomplishment of pertinent tasks. When one studies the history of great industrial families, one almost always comes upon one or more actions of this character—actions on which the family position is founded. Mere husbanding of already existing resources, no matter how painstaking, is always characteristic of a declining position.

In the second case—that of the industrial corporation with trust ramifications—individual success, on the one hand, and family and business success, on the other, do not coincide with the logical necessity that obtains in the case of family enterprises. True, qualifications that foster success vary only in part, may simply develop in other directions; but in the hierarchy of trusts and combinations, types rise that are distinct from those in family enterprises. Only in a relatively small number of cases is family ownership of a majority or even a controlling stock interest possible.[5] Yet without such control an industrialist can run a trust in the manner of an individual plant owner only if he happens to be an altogether extraordinary personality. Even then he will be acting as an individual rather than as a member of a family. In general, this development means the complete displacement of powerful family positions as a typical phenomenon, not merely the shifting of position between families. This is true despite the fact that in cartels proper, with their stabilization of income, family position often seems to be strengthened: at least, observers and often participants as well believe this to be the case—until the next quota is negotiated!

In seeking to understand the factors that account for the success of a corporation official, that lift him above his fellows, we find, first of all, that extraordinary physical and nervous energy have much more to do with outstanding success than is generally believed. It is a simple fact that such industrial leaders must shoulder an often unreasonable burden of current work, which takes up the greater part of the day. They come to their policy-making "conferences" and "negotiations" with different degrees of fatigue or freshness, which have an important bearing on individual success. Moreover, work that opens up new possibilities—the very basis of industrial leadership—falls into the evening and night hours, when few men manage to preserve their full force and originality. With most of them, critical receptivity to new facts has by then given way to a state of exhaustion, and only a few maintain the degree of resolution that leads to decisive action. This makes a great difference the next day. Apart from energy itself, that special kind of "vision" that marks the family entrepreneur also plays an important part—concentration on business to the exclusion of other interests, cool and hard-headed shrewdness, by no means irreconcilable with passion.[6]

In corporate industry it is necessary to woo support, to negotiate with and handle men with consummate skill. Elections and appointments become essential elements in the individual career. These factors are not as prominent in family enterprise, and as a result the standard type of "manager" and "president" is quite different from the proprietary factory entrepreneur of yore. The art of "advancement" counts; the skillful prospers; political connections are of importance; articulateness is an asset. The man who skillfully disposes of a troublesome private matter for an important stockholder need not worry about a bungled shipment. The implications of this situation are the discrepancy between those qualities that enable a man to *reach* a leading position and those that enable him to *hold* it—a discrepancy foreign to family enterprise. There is still another discrepancy, likewise foreign to family enterprise—that between the personal success of the man at the head and the success of the enterprise itself. If this difference does not make itself more strongly felt, this is owing largely to persistence in the class of training in the methods of individually owned business, to which even men who have no such family background are assimilated and disciplined.

We should also mention that rising specialization and

mechanization, reaching right up to the leading functions, has thrown open positions at the top to men with purely technical qualifications that would, of themselves, be inadequate to the needs of family enterprise. A laboratory chemist, for example, may come to head a major chemical enterprise, even though he is not at all the business leader type. A giant industry may be dominated by a lawyer who would push a simple factory to the brink of bankruptcy in no time.

Here too, however, it is always "behavior" and "aptitude" that explain shifts in the relative positions which originally existed. Only in this case, these positions are primarily individual. They affect the family position—by the opportunities opened up, the connections established, and the chances to make money which are presented—but not to the same extent as in the competitive family undertaking. Indeed, in corporate enterprise there is a tendency to evaluate negatively any orientation of leading figures toward personal aggrandizement, to put obstacles in its way, and thus to substitute for the motive of personal profit other motives of a purely personal character—prestige in expert circles, interest in "problems," the urge for action and achievement.

MOVEMENT ACROSS CLASS LINES

7. We have assumed so far that class barriers are insurmountable. This is in accord with a very widespread popular notion that not only governs our evaluation of and emotional reaction to matters in the field of class, but has also gained entry into scientific circles—for the most part only as a half-conscious axiom, attaining the dimensions of an axiomatic rule only in the case of Marxist analysis. The modern radical critique of society often rests on this asserted law, which we must now discuss. There is, of course,

also the question of whether classes as such, without respect to their component elements—their totality, apart from their component cells—endure in perpetuity and in their relative positions, or at least would so endure unless there were upheavals changing the environment. But this question we shall avoid by simply assuming that the answer is affirmative.

It is noncontroversial that the class situation in which each individual finds himself represents a limitation on his scope, tends to keep him within the class. It acts as an obstacle to any rise into a higher class, and as a pair of water wings with respect to the classes below. This is so self-evident that we shall leave it to the reader to enumerate the factors that exert this effect—class type, relations with class fellows, power over outward resources adapted to the class situation, and so on. Whatever historical period, whatever set of social circumstances we may select, we shall always be able to make two assertions that are not likely to be successfully contradicted: In the first place, only in very exceptional cases—so exceptional that they are of no particular significance to the explanation of social processes—is it possible for an individual to enter a "higher" class at a single bound. An example might be a position of sovereignty, achieved by virtue of a coup d'état, affording the usurper immediate entry into the top levels of the aristocratic class.[1] A sudden downfall from the class to which one once belonged, constitutes, so far as I can see, no more than a mischance devoid of basic interest. In the second place, it is *as a rule* practically impossible for the physical individual to effectuate the transition to a higher class *for himself;* and in the overwhelming majority of cases it is impossible for him during his own lifetime to modify decisively the class situation of the true class individual, the family. The occasional cases, however, in which one or the other of these eventualities may occur can no longer be put aside as "basically uninteresting" exceptions.

But it is equally clear, that in our case the relatively short periods under consideration eliminate the phenomenon in question. As soon as we consider longer periods—family histories, for example—the picture becomes different. There we encounter the fundamental fact that classes which in character and relative position must be considered to consist of identical *social* individuals never, in the long run, consist of the same *family* individuals—even if we subtract those that become extinct or drop down to a lower class. On the contrary, there is constant turnover. Entries and exits occur continually—the latter directed both upward and downward. Class composition is forever changing, to the point where there may be a completely new set of families. The rate at which this turnover proceeds varies greatly for different historical periods and social situations. Within each situation it varies for individual classes, and within the latter for individual families. There are cases in which membership in a given class does not even endure for the lifetime of a physical individual; and others in which it lasts for many centuries. Indeed, at first glance such cases of class longevity are unduly prominent, even though they constitute quite rare abnormalities. This difference in the rate of interchange is highly instructive and carries the greatest significance for the verification of our basic idea as well as for an understanding of important social questions. The process always goes on, though at times extremely slowly and almost imperceptibly, impeded by legal and other barriers which every class, for obvious reasons, seeks to erect. For the duration of its collective life, or the time during which its identity may be assumed, each class resembles a hotel or an omnibus, always full, but always of different people.

Precise demonstration of this fact is important not so much as an end in itself—since it can scarcely be disputed—but rather on account of the insight it affords into the rate of social upsurge and decline, and into their causes. Again, we must rest content with a few remarks on the subject. The fact that entry into and exit from a class takes place on an individual basis does not violate the rule that these actions also have their corporative aspect, as it were—that they are of themselves class processes, independent of the behavior of individual families, which indeed, look upon them as "objective" processes. Nevertheless, it will be seen to be the *rule and principle* that entry and exit are *individually effected* by each family. It is not merely a matter of addition and subtraction from a basic stock of families created in some other way; the basic stock itself lives and dies solely by this process of the entry of new families and the exit of old ones. We do not deny that appearances point in the opposite direction. This is always true where a body changes by continual turnover of its parts, arising by continual building up and declining by continual tearing down. At any given moment there is a relatively stable basic stock that seems like a solid core—which it is in a certain sense, but not in the sense that concerns us here.

8. Our demonstration can best be conducted in cases where individual families can be identified and genealogically traced. This is increasingly possible, with the progress that has been made in genealogical research, though there is always likely to be an insurmountable barrier in the dim past. At the present time, really satisfactory material is available only for the aristocracy, notably the high nobility. Sources such as the Golden Book of the Roman aristocracy do offer the evidence we seek. Only a few of the original families were still listed in the seventeenth century, and we can observe precisely how the new names came to be added. In the case of the German high aristocracy, the families, as a rule, cannot be genealogically traced back beyond the year 1200. Yet the broad outlines of the picture emerge, nevertheless. We know, above all from the common law, that at their very entry into history the Germans already had a high nobility that bore the earmarks of a social class. In the case of the Bajuvari, for example, we even know the names of the families. These particular families vanished—in the case of the Bajuvari we later encounter similar names in the ministerial estate—yet a high nobility as such remained. Even earlier, however, new families entered that class, and this happened on a large scale during the Carolingian period, and again under the Ottonians and Salians. We see it more

clearly after the eleventh century, when the documentary evidence for a time distinguishes between names belonging to the high and the low aristocracy. We are able to establish that in the thirteenth century the dividing line between freedom and unfreedom paled, that families that were formerly unfree household officials ascended to the high nobility. Again, by the fifteenth century virtually all the families of the thirteenth-century high aristocracy were extinct or had declined—yet the class lived on. Despite legal and economic fixations, the barriers remained in a state of flux. This is precisely what constitutes the difficult legal problem of "peerage." It is significant for our purposes that there is no clear legal method for defining either the concept or the content of the high nobility as a class—indeed, that the genealogist resists any such attempt. Whenever a family had achieved success, gained wealth and prestige, it was accepted by its superiors, whatever its origin or former status; when it went into a decline, it was suddenly no longer considered to be equal. There were frequent intermediate stages that illustrate this continual process. Occasionally connubium existed between the rising families and those already arrived, though the offspring of such unions still required the formal act of "freeing." But after a while even this requirement lapsed, and any memory of class distinctions ceased. It remained true that the more firmly class position was established, the more difficult it was to surmount the barriers. Yet they *were* surmounted time and again, after the fifteenth century as well as before. The great Austrian families of German blood, for example, sprang almost exclusively from the ministerial estate. And more and more, proven service to the sovereign became the key that opened the door to the circles of the high nobility. Just as that class continually gained recruits from the class of knights, so this class replenished itself, down to the eleventh century, from the peasant class. Until then there was no legal barrier to prevent the peasant from becoming a "knight." All he needed to do was to secure a mount and arms, and to prove his worth in battle. Whoever reached this economic estate and demonstrated his usefulness in war service, normally received a "service" fief, and though this was not the equivalent of "genuine" enfeoffment, it established his identification with the warlike master class. This particular procedure lapsed more and more, because the technical qualifications of knights steadily rose from the twelfth to the fifteenth centuries, and because the established class grew more "firm." But that does not affect our principle. And the cases of the "bourgeois knight" and the "knightly bourgeois" are analogous.

But when we make the leap to the industrial world of capitalism, the lack of genealogical material becomes even more keenly felt. True, such data are being accumulated, if only under the spur of modern genealogical interest as such; but the lack of zeal with which social scientists gather and evaluate this material is in lamentable contrast to the fact that it alone can provide a reliable knowledge of the structure and life processes of capitalist society. Only a fundamental indifference to scientific problems as such can explain the slow progress of social science, a fact which is nowhere more obvious than here, where nearly everyone is satisfied with party slogans. We do have, nevertheless, a considerable number of histories covering industrial, intellectual, and even working-class families. A beginning has also been made in preparing collections of family histories. One such collection, by Professor Haensels (Moscow), exceeds a thousand entries.[2] The picture that emerges is uniformly along the lines of the American saying: "Three generations from shirtsleeves to shirtsleeves." To an even greater degree it bears out our thesis, that the content of every "upper" class is not merely *modified* but actually *formed* by the rise and decline of individual families; and that the demonstrable transgression of class barriers is not the exception but so much the invariable rule in the life of every upper-class family that despite certain variations in detail, we are not likely to meet with great surprises.

The most interesting question, of course, is to what extent industrial families are recruited directly from the working class and, to that extent, form no more than the upper layer of that class. (In this connection it is best to avoid the term "elite" which is often and without justification used in the sense of a positive evaluation.) An ordinary census will serve to answer this question, and we have Chapman to thank for such an inquiry.[3] He studied the English cotton industry and found that between 63 and 85 per cent of the entrepreneurs and other leaders had risen directly from the working class (that is, the results of the various subinquiries lay between these limits). True, the factual basis was narrow, the methods were imperfect, though painstaking and praiseworthy for a first step. The textile industry, moreover—especially the English textile industry—is not typical. But for our purposes the size of the percentage etsablished by Chapman is not necessary—10 per cent would have been entirely sufficient, provided it could be demonstrated that the *ancestors* of the remaining 90 per cent had similarly risen from the working or other classes. Even then the theory of an "objective" bond between family and class would have been proved redundant. In other words, the worker, for example, would be objectively tied to his class only in the sense that he ceases to be a "worker" when he deserts his class.[4]

9. We see therefore that our earlier assumption as to the insurmountability of class barriers for individual families does not accord with the facts. The persistence of class position is an illusion, created by the slowness of change and the great stability of class character as such and of its social fluid. Class barriers *must* be surmountable, at the bottom as well as at the top. Otherwise how explain that at sufficiently distinct points in time we always find different people in classes that are identical as such, just as we deal forever with different individuals in families that nevertheless remain identical? Like the birth and death of individual family members, which are always events that transcend the everyday course of events and thus constitute something exceptional, entry into and exit from a class appear to us as special and in *this* sense exceptional events; but in *another*

sense they are entirely normal. We see, therefore, that families *do* surmount class barriers, as *individuals* rather than as a class—though quite often in groups—and that they do this in a manner which we can, even today, study in a sufficient number of individual cases, as well as in all important groups of cases. But this process does not yet explain the formation of classes as such. It does explain, as already stated, not only the gradual *modification* of the basic family stock in a class which might have been created in some other way, but also the *formation* of whatever stock exists at a given point in time. *Only the physical individual, not the family, is class-born.*

The question of *how* this process of surmounting class barriers takes place and why class content changes now answers itself. Primarily it happens precisely as does the shifting of position of individual families within the class. It is only necessary to examine the reasons for those shifts which we have cited in order to see at once that they are quite adequate to account for the rise and fall of individual families not only within the class but also between classes. The family in question only needs to be near the upper or lower border line of its class, and the factors that account for shifts to be strong enough to surmount the barriers peculiar to classes. These barriers are not really different in kind, only in strength, from those that limit the rise or decline of families within the class. It is seen at once that these factors actually do account for the rise or fall of a family above or below its class barriers. As a rule, such changes occur imperceptibly. Only where law or custom confers on members of certain classes certain formal qualifications—such as special political privileges or the right to perform certain religious ceremonies—is there a recognizable outward act that can be dated. And in such cases one might actually be led to believe that it is not so much a matter of voluntary ascent as a process of being pushed up the ladder from the outside. This, however, is not so. Even in such cases it is actually a matter of growth, of first creating a position which is then recognized to be a fact, in the face of which such acts as admission and appointment are merely corroborative. It is apparent that the admission of certain families to the councils of counts [*Grafenkollegien*] in the seventeenth and eighteenth centuries did not *establish* the social position of those families but were merely *expressive* of that position—although it is equally clear that such action *did* qualify the families in question for membership in those councils and for the rather insignificant privileges linked to such membership. The heart of the matter is much more clearly expressed in the essentially similar process during the Middle Ages in which a family was actually received into the circle of princely lieges, with no particular formal ceremony. The fact that certain barriers may have actually been insurmountable for centuries on end becomes a special reason why there should be no special ritual act governing the acceptance of new families. But this is the case only where ethnic differences exist—the Indian caste system is the outstanding example—and has nothing to do with the essential nature of the class phenomenon.

Yet there *is* an apparently new element, entirely absent in shifts within the class, the significance of which must be sought here. Apart from favorable or unfavorable accidents, we have considered it to be the rule, in cases of ascent or descent within the class, that the class member performs with more or less success than his fellows those activities that he must perform in any event, that are chosen by or imposed on him within his class limitations. For example, a member of a military or priestly master class may have more success than his fellows with his feuds or prophecies; a tailor may serve his customers better than other tailors; the professional may win a larger number of cases or cure a larger number of patients than other lawyers or doctors. But there is, of course, still another way that is particularly apposite to the transgression of class barriers. That is to *do something altogether different* from what is, as it were, ordained to the individual. The knight may become a statesman or administrator; the cleric may suddenly enhance the standing of his family by virtue of a career in the service of the Papal See—as a study of papal nepotism down to the end of the eighteenth century shows; artisan families like the Wurmsers and Fuggers may develop into great merchant dynasties; the modern worker may, in familiar fashion, push his son into the so-called new middle class, or, as we have seen, himself become an entrepreneur—which does not, of itself, *constitute* class position, but *leads* to class position.

Reverting to the element of chance for a moment, the likelihood of lucky accidents naturally increases when position is enhanced for other reasons, a circumstance which constitutes the other aspect of the relationship between luck and ability. The first and most important aspect we have already mentioned. Family and social history show that, in addition to the elements of chance and success along wonted and ordained lines, the method of rising into a higher class which we are now discussing is of crucial importance—the method of striking out along unconventional paths. This has always been the case, but never so much as in the world of capitalism. True, many industrial families, especially in the middle brackets, have risen from small beginnings to considerable or even great wealth by dint of hard work and unremitting attention to detail over several generations; but most of them have come up from the working and craftsman class—to a lesser degree, and then only indirectly, from the peasantry (I pass over the transition of members of the free professions to industry, because this does not necessarily imply transgression of a class barrier)—because one of their members has *done something novel,* typically the founding of a new enterprise, something that meant getting out of the conventional rut. Because of the limited opportunities open to working-class families, this is virtually the only method by which they can make the great leap out of their class.

Even though this is another and different way of rising, the conditions under which a family can follow it with success are, from our viewpoint, no different from those under which position is enhanced within the class. This statement applies only to our own viewpoint, for from other viewpoints and for other purposes it is often relevant that the method *is* a different one, that to move with assurance outside the rut, to do something special that has not been done before in essentially similar fashion, requires different qualities. This latter aspect of launching out into the unprecedented is not, by the way, necessarily implied in every case, though it does play a part in certain important cases and is basically significant to our further line of reasoning. For the present we may say that the capacity and ability to rise socially along this second line requires nothing more than a stronger endowment with the same or similar qualifications that bring success along the first line. *Those factors that account for shifts in family position within the class are the same that account for the crossing of class barriers.*

THE RISE AND FALL OF WHOLE CLASSES

10. We observe, furthermore, that the class structure of a people also changes by virtue of the fact that the relative social position of the classes as such undergoes shifts. A question now poses itself that is analogous to the question concerning the reasons for shifts of individual families within the class. Why and how do classes change their relative position?

We see such a shift most plainly, not in cases where it is the result of a slow, organic process, but in those where it occurs by a single historical event. The most important instance of the latter process is the forcible subjugation of one social entity by another that is politically alien—usually nationally as well, though that is not essential to us now. What interests us in such an upheaval is the fact that classes that appear as "upper" or "ruling" even to superficial observation—especially *the* "ruling class"—are much more deeply affected than the "lower" classes, and in an altogether different way. True, even the lower classes may often—though not always or necessarily—be put in a worse economic plight, but their position as a class, their relative social rating, is affected only slightly or not at all, usually remaining essentially unchanged under the new overlord. The upper classes, on the other hand, are likely to lose the very core of their position—the more so, the nearer they are to the top of the social pyramid. Let us, for example, take the conquest of certain Romanized regions by the Germans during the Great Migration. The Romanized strata of the provinces of Rhaetia and Noricum, for example, usually became so-called *tributarii*—peasants compelled to offer tribute, though not necessarily unfree. As an alternative, they might keep one part of their property, if they surrendered the rest. By and large, this probably corresponded to the position the same people occupied down to the final period under Rome. Similarly, we find certain Slavs who had been tenants even under the Avari continuing in the same state under Germanic rule, while others in Carinthia and Pannonia, who had fared better before, continued as free landowners. But the situation of the upper class was severely depressed, even where the class continued to maintain itself. The position of Roman citizens of the highest class in these same regions was characterized by the fact that persons who had not been free before but were now manumitted *per cartam ingenuitatis* were declared to be their equals, while the *denariales* actually stood above them. True, these were primarily legal distinctions, but they must be considered symptoms of an altered class position. Among the above-mentioned Slavs, for example, the native aristocracy did succeed in maintaining itself, in a regime that remained largely autonomous, but it no longer carried the weight it once did. There is only one way in which the upper class can maintain its full social position under such circumstances; that is when it is received into the corresponding class of the conqueror. In our cases this came about through the cession of lands to the king and in general it occurs quite frequently. Thus it was a common policy of the East Roman Empire to accept the nobility of subjugated peoples (of Bulgaria, for example, in the time of the Macedonian emperors) into the imperial Byzantine nobility. But it will be seen at once that this constitutes no exception to our assertion; for it was not the old class itself that retained its social validity, but merely the sum of its members in their function as members of what now came to be the upper class.

Yet even this shift in the relative position of the classes toward each other does not quite tell us what we need to know. After all, it was the result of outside influence, which was accidental from the viewpoint of the class system in existence before. Let us, nevertheless, take note of the following two elements: to be conquered always means failure, and the failure applies particularly to the ruling classes. Apparently it is this inherent character of subjugation, so destructive to prestige, that has, in turn, much to do with the forfeiture of social position. A calamity lacking this special character—a great earthquake, for example—would not have such an effect, unless it were linked in the public mind with a failure, on the part of the upper classes, to entertain, let us say, good relations with the gods. This offers an obvious analogy with the effect of personal failure of a leader—a leader of mounted nomads, for example.[1] The position of a monarchial family is typically rooted in class. Yet nothing shakes its position so much as an unsuccessful war. It would be difficult to find any case of loss of monarchial position that did not have, at least indirectly, some connection with this element. Again, this matter of having been subjugated or of meeting with failure is not just a question of failure in general, failure in any field; the failure becomes relevant only when it occurs with respect to certain definite fields—not merely those fields which the observer, from the necessities he has grasped, deems important, but those for which the class in question is responsible in a way that other classes are not. Only when a class has thus been weighed and found wanting, in the light of the circumstances of the times, does its position toward other classes of citizens decline—all down the line, not merely in this point alone—although, of course, a position once gained may prove equal to quite a number of such tests.

11. Here, then, in a flash, we begin to see the underlying relationship that leads directly to an answer to our question. This is the connection between the social rank of a class and its function. Each class is always linked to such a special function. That is the real core of all theories of the division of labor and occupation in the field of class phenomena— except that these theories, in our opinion, evaluate this element incorrectly. (For this reason I ask the reader, in the interest of avoiding troublesome misunderstandings, to impute to our line of reasoning no part of the content of those theories, indeed, if possible, to put them out of his mind.) Every class, in other words, has a definite function, which it must fulfill according to its whole concept and orientation, and which it actually does discharge as a class and through the class conduct of its members. Moreover, the position of each class in the total national structure, depends, on the one hand, on the significance that is attributed to that function, and, on the other hand, on the degree to which the class successfully performs the function. Changes in relative class position are always explained by changes along these two lines, and in no other way. For the time being, the propositions just put forth are liable to obvious objections. Just what their meaning is will be shown by an example which at the same time may serve to demonstrate our line of reasoning for cases that are not dependent on the effect of outside forces. The proof cannot be absolute, for that would require an analysis of universal history.

First of all, let us record the instructive fact that there are two groups of cases in which class structure is only very weakly marked. An example of the first group is furnished by the Slavs during the time they lived in the Pripet marshes. We must envision them as subdivided into very small communities, isolated by the difficult terrain, leading a highly stable existence, with untoward events quite infrequent and opportunities at home exceedingly narrow. Such dangers as did exist—invasions by Germanic or Mongol bandits and slavers—were, given the situation and the character of the people, practically beyond control. They could not be guarded against in advance. Flight was the only recourse—into some hiding place, possibly even below the water, with a hollow reed for a breathing tube. It is clear why there were no more than traces of class structure here. There was no opportunity, no occasion for class leadership. Class distinctions and social differentiations arise and have meaning only where environmental factors change with sufficient speed, where there is scope for action, decision, and service. It is different with the other group of cases, typified by the mounted nomad. Life on the steppe with its plundering forays is marked by constant change. The very physical environment alternates rapidly. The situation is always essentially new and it becomes a matter of choosing, acting, winning—or perishing. Hence individual differentiation is strongly marked. The leadership function is strongly marked, the leadership position well developed. Yet here too there are only feeble hints of class structure, even though it is much stronger than in the first group of cases. What class structure there is consists essentially of the fact that the prestige of the leaders—which is primarily graduated by their success and built up of individual successes—when once present, elevates the leader's personal circle, permitting those born into it to start with better chances than other members of the community. But all adult men are simply warriors and within the whole group—which cannot live by itself alone, in the long run always needing a host people to exploit—there are no distinguishable social functions, except for the leadership function as such. Hence we never find strongly developed stable class positions in such cases—either among the Mongol and Semitic mounted nomads, or, for example, among the Eskimos. Now let us examine our example.

12. At the time the Germans entered the limelight of history, their aristocracy was no more than the leading circle of

a mounted nomad people. It was simply a circle of families of enhanced prestige—more precisely, a plurality of distinct circles, differing from one another by the degree of prestige they enjoyed. Their members had more to do with making the policies of the totality than the rest. They were more closely associated with such action as had to be taken, with such benefits as accrued. It is important to emphasize that this was relative rather than absolute, that the situation remained basically in a state of flux. There were real or potential chieftains of larger or smaller groups and subgroups. Yet there was one distinction as against the case of the mounted nomads, a distinction which explains the sharply marked character of the picture. Even when we first catch sight of them, the Germans were in a very high stage of agriculture, normally and preeminently living by tilling the soil. True, in *all* the German tribes this characteristic could be temporarily subordinated during migrations, and with *some* of them this was permanently the case, by virtue of special circumstances, especially when a tribe, or part of a tribe, was in a position to lead a life of banditry, or established itself as the ruling class in some foreign land. Agriculture, to a much higher degree than nomadic animal husbandry, destroys uniformity of behavior among the members of a community,[2] and *adds a new distinction to that between leaders and led.* Hence we encounter the Germanic aristocracy from the very outset in a more sharply circumscribed special function. We need scarcely fear contradiction when we characterize this function as that of military leadership—a leadership, however, that meant not merely the command of forces but, to an increasing degree during the ensuing centuries, the actual execution of combat actions. Nor need we fear contradiction when we assert that this is the primary explanation for the generally enhanced position of the aristocracy, for its association with further functions —presiding at group meetings, leadership in other group concerns. It is plausible that the predominance of the military function, in uncomplicated circumstances and where the group is small in numbers, inhibits the emergence of positions of a different character. In the course of the Great Migrations and the concluding Merovingian and Carolingian successes, this social class steadily rose in power and position—it is of small moment, in this connection, that actual family content may have turned over rather rapidly. There can be no doubt, after all, that we are still entitled to speak of the same class. The question now at issue is no sooner put than answered. How can we explain this rise,[3] this shift in relative class position? Evidently from the fact that, in the circumstances of the time, the basic class function gained in actual importance—as understood by us, the observers—and that this importance was sensed, not necessarily consciously, by the rest of the people. Both aspects are essential. Without the former there would not, in the long run, be an adequate explanation, a link with the objective facts of life of the social group; without the latter the vital connections between those vital facts and the phenomenon they created would be lacking.

This enhanced importance is *reflected and objectified* in the rise of a definite institution among the Germans in their new territories—the creation of great manorial estates. This is their social meaning and they become incomprehensible when this element is left out of consideration. It is for this very reason that the problem of the rise of such estates is such a complex and controversial one in the literature of legal and social history. All of a sudden, as it were, the great estates are in existence in the Carolingian period. One can only conclude from this fact that far-reaching social transformations had taken place; and, as is often the case with problems that are more apparent than real, this one has given rise to labored theories that are not always free of unconscious humor. Actually it is no more than the expression and gradual realization of an administrative system that arose independently, under the impact of our factor of a previously shifted class structure. Like the feudal system itself, the manorial estates, in one of their aspects, are only the expression of an administrative system adapted to special outward circumstances and the special class structure of the times—to the legal system in general, to passive methods of disposing of natural resources. (The methods are not necessarily passive in every case.) With the establishment of the great estates and the development of a mode of life in keeping with their conception at the time, as well as of a body of law affecting all classes—vassalage, immunity, court privilege, village law, and so on—there commenced a great social process that was subject to many fluctuations and setbacks and that ended only in the nineteenth century with the complete abolition of manorial privileges, even then leaving a heritage of established position to later times. We shall call this process *patrimonialization.*

13. There are four factors that justify the proposition that, down to the threshold of the "modern age," the relative position of our class was rising rather than sinking. I think this is apparent from the fact that, for the most part, its actual and legal privileges were on the increase, while similarly those of the remaining classes were on the decline. The only exception in this respect is the urban bourgeoisie, even though its rise did not take place in a straight line. It did, however, demonstrate the ultimate impotence of legal and political restrictions, even when the outward resources of power are at the disposal of those that impose them. It burst out of the social pyramid of feudal society, slipped from the grasp of the nobility, and enhanced its own weight and function despite all class legislation.

True, in the course of the centuries there were radical upheavals within that other class. (Technically, we should really speak in the plural, or at least distinguish between high and low aristocracy, but for the sake of simplicity in presentation we shall here speak only of a single class of feudal lords.) There were numerous shifts in the position of groups within the class—above all, a constant turnover of its constituents. There were losses as well as gains in all these respects, though in the long run the gains outweighed the losses, as far as concerns class position as such. This outcome is attributable to the following four reasons: In the first place, during this entire time war essentially retained its character as a mode of life—a character it has since increasingly lost. It was a normal thing, not a last resort, as it came to be later. War and instant readiness for war remained an indispensable element of survival in every walk of life, in all socially characteristic situations. Those who could not themselves function along these lines were dependent on the protection of some individual warlord. Because this class function was so vital, it served to enhance the significance of another factor we should like to adduce in explaining shifts in class position. The class in question exercised its function with signal success. For, in the second place, the warrior of that period grew into an expert mounted fighter.[4] Success in the profession of arms required not merely an aptitude for fighting, but constant application to technical mastery. Those who had other concerns were by that fact alone disqualified from the full exercise of this function. Today, special technical skill can be confined to the few who, in case of need, can in a short time train men drawn from their regular occupations. But that was not true then. Nor could the military rest content with working out measures for mobilization. The warlord himself constituted the machine on which everything rested. These circumstances lie at the very heart of the matter. It was no mere whim of Charles Martel that brought into being the mounted host of knights, any more than the feudal system was born of his campaigns against the Arabs. Fortunately it has at last been recognized that both phenomena merely expressed environmental and structural changes the beginnings of which can already be seen in the early Germanic period. This also disposes of the seemingly plausible notion that possession of certain "means of production"—horse and armor—was the factor that led to the formation of the class. It is only necessary to realize that one of the objectives of the system of benefices must have been to furnish not only these immediate means but also those required for the life and profession of a knight in general to those who had already been chosen for other reasons. Yet these material elements and the way in which they were provided did have the effect of elevating and securing class position. There were other mere consequences that worked in the same direction. On the one hand, the class base was broadened. Even relatively, the number of professional warriors was greater than that of the members of the nobility in the time of universal liability to military service. Then again, the qualities required and developed by the chivalric life were eminently suited to the defense of class position against other segments of the population, which in turn were in the process of losing these very qualities. A third reason for rising class position lay in the elaboration of functions that were originally subsidiary to the main function but that now, by virtue of the situation, were carefully preserved and even more closely associated with it. National horizons, interests, and tasks were expanding, and the upper class found ever new sources of activity and thus of power in the great problems of empire, which assumed reality for it alone. It should be pointed out, however, that the situation is by no means exhaustively characterized by mere reference to the interrelationship of these functions with the basic function that genetically explains class position. Two other relationships must be considered and conceptually differentiated from the one described. Quite apart from the fact that aptitude for war was necessary even for the exercise of these further functions—a qualification that gradually disappeared —it is manifestly significant that the exercise of these other functions was objectively related to the military preoccupations of a person of high rank. Here too it was a matter of deciding, commanding, leading, winning. This the knights— or at least a sufficient number of them—were able and willing to do. It was from their ranks that the emerging high nobility was recruited, and by no means exclusively nor even normally from the families of the earlier high nobility; and it was this section of the knighthood that maintained and enhanced the position of the entire knightly class. No such interrelationship was apparent in the economic sphere. The knight had neither the desire nor the ability to become a trader. Later on, as we shall presently see, this was reversed, though only in a special sense—a fact which again justifies our conception and explains the emergence of the bourgeois from the feudal class structure, as well as the already mentioned relative decline of the nobility as against this new group whose ancestors had once stood far beneath the nobility, whether they had been legally subordinate or not. The fundamental significance of this relationship to class development is evident, and it will later be formulated in general terms. Another relationship exists by virtue of the fact that, quite apart, for the moment, from the two correlations described, members of an elevated class, especially when their position has materialized even outwardly into privileges, property, and organic functions, find easier access to new functions (which they may even monopolize) than members of other classes. A fourth reason for the rise in the position of our class lies in the opportunities it had to colonize frontier regions, either for its own benefit or at any rate for the benefit of small subgroups, in its capacity to exploit these opportunities, and in the fact that they *were* exploited with success. This led to rising wealth, to a position of dominance over aliens, which in turn enhanced class position at home.[5]

14. Yet from the end of the fourteenth century down to the present day our class has been almost without interruption on the downgrade. This is seen not so much in its legal status which even gained rather than lost in the fifteenth, sixteenth, and seventeenth centuries and did not begin to be systematically undermined until the eighteenth century— which agrees with the general observation that of all the clearly marked elements of social life the "super-structure" [6] of law, custom, and so forth is always the last to change, always lags behind changes in the actual life situation. Nor is it expressed in a decline in "social" position which, on the contrary, has been surprisingly well maintained to the present day. Rather does this decline emerge in the invariable subjection of the class to a new social factor—new, at least, in this particular form—the state power. At first glance it may seem as though this holds nothing new from the view-

point of our subject, as though this need not impinge on class position as such. For primarily the "state power" meant no more than the sum total of the powers of the sovereign; and subjection of this nature meant no more than subjection to a superior within the class. On the one hand, such subordination lay in the very nature of the feudal system. On the other hand, in our view any great enhancement of the sovereign position, insofar as it elevated the sovereign as against the rest of the nobility, would be irrelevant to the position of the class as such; while, insofar as the sovereign was elevated with respect to other classes, it should have enhanced the position of the nobility as a whole. But the fact is that the sovereign did not subjugate the nobility in his capacity as feudal overlord; he did so in his capacity as master over an entirely different power—and it was to this power that he bent the nobility. There arose an administrative machine, at first predominantly manned by the nobility—more of this presently—but one with which it was by no means identical. This machinery, being capable of functioning equally well and even better in other hands, could be—and was in fact—wrested from the grasp of the nobility and even of the sovereign. Objectively and theoretically, this was a new kind of subordination—submission to something that *ultimately turned out to be alien and even hostile.*

What we mean by patrimonialization is the process that explains this unfavorable change in class position—a process that must itself be explained. The term, in other words, is used in a broader sense than its technical application in legal and social history. We mean, first of all, the familiar process by which, from the Carolingian period on, vital functions became hereditary. Briefly, imperfectly, and indeed incorrectly[7] put, they tended to become objects of the law of property. This is the *patrimonialization of office.* Secondly, we mean the process by which landownership by the nobles became—at first in fact and then in law (in its extreme form this is the alodification of fiefs)—a thing apart from the unified feudal system, in time simply a source of income, a means of production, an object of traffic. This is the *patri-*

monialization of landed property. Thirdly, we mean the process by which the individual emerged from the obligations and attitudes of the feudal relationship, becoming in theory a citizen left to his own devices, shaping his private sphere more or less at will, even though for the time being he was still invested with special privileges and tied to fixed social forms. This is the *patrimonialization of the individual.* The rococo period shows us an intermediate state that is highly illuminating. In many outward respects the position of the nobility was never more splendid. Socially, legally, and materially, it rested on the very extensive heritage of the feudal age, in part well preserved, for the rest showing itself highly resistant even in a state of impairment. In all three directions this position was strengthened by the fact that the new state machine, whatever it may have taken away from the old position of overlordship, still needed to be staffed by the nobility, while in financial respects it proved at first to be an almost inexhaustible object of exploitation. What the historian, often quite superficially, describes as courtly extravagance at the whim of the sovereign was actually the very essence of a social and political system which sought to transform the nobility from an independent gentry into a pliant court aristocracy, not merely by force but also by economic temptation. Actually the time of that independence, when the nobles stood on their own two feet, was at end. The essence and guarantee of independence had lain in the fact that in case of need the lord would mount his horse and defend himself, sword in hand, against dangers from above or below—the last example, already adulterated by other factors, is furnished by the sixteenth-century peasant wars. The time was past when the coronation formula of Aragon was a striking expression of an actual situation, when the concept of the "peer" had real meaning. Now the servility of the estates just as strikingly expressed a new situation of dependence on the favor and protection of the state machine. More and more the position of overlordship became a derivate, even where it antedated the state and had its foundations outside the state, even though it continued to enjoy the glory of ancient—and otherwise to n increasing degree borrowed—associations. In telling confirmation of our view, the complement to this situation was that the lower nobility was primarily preoccupied with its private concerns, while the higher nobility as such had nothing whatever to do. The facts are in part obscured by the circumstance that *members* of both groups were active in the service of the state, while there was an understandable tendency to continue the old functions in form rather than in substance. The rugged pugnacity of the knight remained as an ideal, to be refined into the fine arts of wielding the foil and riding according to the tenets of the classical school, utterly devoid of any further significance in the social struggle for survival. Intervention in the affairs of state became a skillful ritual, an end in itself without relevance to the task in hand. If the action had any meaning at all, this was determined, not by the great lords who actually figured in the proceedings, but by other persons and interests. It is this survival of social and material position on the one hand, and the extensive decay of underlying functions on the other, that explain the characteristic charm and high culture of that period. True, even then this group had not completely closed ranks, but it had far fewer motives for accepting newcomers than any class immediately embroiled in the struggle for survival where it must stand up and show its mettle. Yet for a while, during the time in question, the nobility could utterly ignore the nature of the relationship between ruling and serving, could temporarily surrender to the illusion that the world was its oyster, that fun was the only purpose of life, that any act that was not pure entertainment represented a graciously conferred boon. All classes, including the ruling class, exercise rights just for the sake of maintaining them. But the rococo period was characterized by the exercise of rights (which were more and more losing their function) for purely selfish reasons—and this meant that the overlord really ceased to be one, in the essential meaning of his class position. Obviously the course of events in the eighteenth century supports our contention that such a situation could continue only because it was the heritage of an altogether different situation, and also because it never existed in the pure state and was always subject to numerous corrective and weakening factors. The only alternatives would have been a timely, voluntary surrender or adaptation to a process marked by legal continuity, or loss of position by events that break such continuity—in other words, retreat or defeat; and both contingencies lead to the same final result.[8]

15. To the degree required for our purposes, we may enumerate the essential elements and causes of the process of patrimonialization under the four headings we have set forth. The scope of our study requires, however, that in each case we rest content with only the first links in causal chains that ultimately reach very deep. Thus we cannot immediately discuss why physical, armed combat ceased to be a mode of life inside the national community, and gradually outside it as well. But the fact that this happened did pull the foundation from under the main function of our class. One has only to ask oneself whether the competitive economy of the nineteenth century could have existed if industrial families had not had to be continually concerned over their survival and to give constant attention to current business decisions. Reflection will show why we assert that the occasional exercise of a function—no matter how frequent the occasion, how vital the preoccupation, how suitable the function to become the basis of a full-time vocation—is insufficient to intrench a special discipline and orientation in such a way that they become the very life of a class. Even when he serves in the army, the modern conscript remains at heart a civilian. The modern professional soldier is a soldier in the sense that a lawyer is a lawyer. He is *not* a warrior, even though the traditional officer corps, in order to engender or preserve such an orientation, cultivates a warrior ideology, even going so far as to keep alive the fiction of individual readiness for combat by tolerating or promoting the duel. But when combat is no longer a mode of life, when it is no longer imminent at any moment in defense of

immediate, personal interests—then it is no longer *the* great task, foreordained and self-evident. Battle, even though it may still be frequent, soon becomes an emergency situation, foreign and disturbing to other spheres of life, and there is no longer occasion for every member of the class to be constantly trained in it with every fiber of his being. This carries two consequences. The basic cause for the slow demilitarization of the nobility must be sought in the whole trend of society, which more and more circumscribed the occasion and opportunity for defending individual and class position by force of arms. Ultimately this demilitarization made the armed class struggle—if one wishes to use that term—altogether impossible, and thus one of the conspicuous guarantees of class position fell by the wayside. Of far greater importance was the fact that this demilitarization, and the resulting orientation toward other interests, more and more had the effect of turning the nobility against its own basic function, causing it to undermine the very foundations of its own social importance. To an ever-increasing degree military service was rejected. It was not that the obligation to render such service was denied, but it was regarded as onerous and the call to it was complied with only grudgingly, if at all. Proof is furnished by the fact that in the fifteenth and early sixteenth centuries the feudal lords used the call to military service as one of the ways of making the estates comply with their financial requirements—something that can be understood only when it is realized that such duty, while acknowledged, was also resented. In this way, a replacement was found for the nobility in that sphere where combat still remained vital to survival—a sphere in which the nobility might well have continued to play a role, preserving part of its social importance. We should not overrate the significance of technical innovations in this process. On the technical side there was nothing to keep the nobility from taking to small arms and ordnance, just as it had once, with similar social results, mastered the technique of mounted and armored combat. It is no valid objection to say that the new techniques led to an increase in the number of effectives. For apart from the fact that this was to a certain extent a consequence of the circumstance that the people replacing the nobility were available in greater numbers, the earlier introduction of the host of mounted knights had itself led to a numerical increase in the nobility, a process to which any class vigorously oriented toward its function readily submits. *It is only because this did not happen now* that we think of the nobility as clinging stubbornly to the fighting methods of the Middle Ages and that the very idea of the nobility's adapting itself to the new methods seems far-fetched and unreal. Yet the army of knighthood did not fail because the mercenary army came into being. Rather the system of mercenaries arose because the knightly host failed from inner causes. But once the new situation existed, once the mercenary system functioned—with the nobility in part furnishing the financial resources (though mostly from the pockets of its own copyholders) for the very purpose of evading military service—*then* the army of knighthood had really grown obsolete and inferior. There was a stronger power in existence now, and this meant a fundamental change in the total social-class structure. As we shall presently have occasion to discuss again, the individual knight was still the most likely candidate for positions of leadership in the mercenary army; and significantly enough, he endeavored for a long time, by his bearing and appearance, to convey the impression that he was prepared at any moment to ride out full tilt with lowered lance to meet the enemy in individual combat—though in the end he was likely to don armor only when his portrait was to be painted. Even though this shed glamor on the class as a whole, it was something rather different from bearing the whole burden of combat. Yet the survival of such conspicuous externals served to slow down the full effect of the internal change. And with this, we have disposed not only of the first two of the four factors we enumerated as effecting changes in position, but also of the fourth, since the possibility of private colonization is obviously associated with the warrior function as a whole.

16. The process by which our class relinquished its basic class function implies not merely voluntary surrender and failure of will power, but also the pressure of the objective social situation which resulted in inactivity and flagging will. It implies not only *giving up,* but also, once that had begun, *taking away.* For the nobles this process was at the same time a process of individual emancipation, and it enabled the nobility as a class to loosen all the other feudal bonds— bonds which had already begun to lose meaning and to enter into a state of atrophy. This is just what we mean, in the case of the nobility, by "patrimonialization of the individual." But it is precisely because a decline in the social importance of a class function—the inadequate exercise and ultimate surrender of that function—*sets the members of the class free* that the decline in class position which might be expected occurs only if the class is unable to adapt itself to some other function that rates the same social importance as the old one. This fact, let us remark in passing, constitutes a severe limitation on the explanatory value of the relationship between class and function. There can never be any lack of new functions, unless a people chances into a stagnant social situation, free of problems. And every class that has once enjoyed an elevated position is greatly aided in seizing on new functions, because the sources and gains of its prior function survive for some time. In our own case we see at once that two such functions automatically obtruded themselves on the nobility by virtue of their relation to its former position as the warrior and master class, and to which it did, in fact, turn. These functions were the staffing of the state machine and the administration of its own landed estates. It is at once evident why these two functions were, on the one hand, able to slow down and soften the descent of the class, while, on the other hand, they were insufficient to preserve its old position. Orientation toward individually owned landed property did not occur everywhere at the same rate and in the same manner. The differences in this respect are highly instructive. Where the state machine arose on the basis of the princely domain [*Fürstenter-*

ritorium]—which was the case precisely where the mercenary system was most strongly developed—this orientation
took place much more rapidly and sharply than in cases
where the state had other antecedents, the single important
example of the latter being England. Longer than anywhere
else, and to a certain extent down to the present day, the
English nobility continued in a position of national leadership, though in the course of time it became an agent rather
than a ruler. It was able to do so because it did not turn to
agriculture as an occupation and thus, on the one hand, remained free of all economic activity, while, on the other, it
never degenerated into a group of economic and political
partisans, as the nobility of other countries did. Nevertheless, the causes, the broad outlines, and the ultimate results
of the process were everywhere the same, except that they
emerge with particular clarity where the nobleman turns
husbandman, where landlordism develops in its pure form.
*Just as the manorial system corresponds to the type of the
knightly warrior-politician and warrior-administrator, so the
system of large landed estates corresponds to the type of
the aristocratic businessman.* Naturally our process was determined by economic developments. Landlordism is possible only when population density has risen and when centers of consumption exist. The declining purchasing power
of feudal money rents was a sharp incentive to the exploitation of inherited feudal resources for private economic gain,
even though such exploitation was destructive of prestige.
But the heart of the matter lies in the conquests of the period between the Merovingians and Hohenstaufens, which
led to a situation in which the administration and enjoyment of what had been gained, individually and as a class,
made for a full life, weakening the incentive for further
headlong action—quite apart from the fact that outward opportunities for such action began to dwindle. These developments gave a calculating, private-economic direction to
the nobility's attitude toward such matters as its own property, its relation to the peasantry, and the maintenance of
feudal rights and duties. And all this, in turn, led to cor-

responding legal forms and constitutes the social content of the "patrimonialization of landed property."

17. The situation is basically similar in the case of the "patrimonialization of office." It too becomes comprehensible from the same causal nexus. Here too, in the course of time, the successful families established themselves in the positions they had temporarily acquired, as though such a situation must automatically endure—just as the bourgeoisie in the early nineteenth century established itself in the positions it had created, invested those positions with appropriate legal standing, regarded individual control of the means and fruits of production as self-evident and, indeed, the whole order as permanent, because it was "natural." Yet this analogy does not extend all the way. It deserts us because of the circumstance that the old overlords, in order to administer and maintain their position, did not always have to repeat those actions that had led to the conquest of that position, while the position of the industrialists is rapidly dissipated unless it is constantly marked by the same kind of success that created it. That is the main reason why the analogy between feudal and industrial rule breaks down when applied seriously and in detail. There are, to be sure, other reasons as well, of which we shall mention the two most important. The feudal master class was once—and the bourgeoisie was never—the supreme pinnacle of a uniformly constructed social pyramid. The feudal nobility was once lord and master in every sphere of life—which constitutes a difference in prestige that can never be made up. Moreover, the feudal nobility was once—and the bourgeoisie was never —not only the sole possessor of physical power; it *was* physical power incarnate. The aforementioned main difference, however, means, on the one hand, that in the case of the nobility, class and individual family position endured far better and longer than in the case of the bourgeoisie. It means, on the other hand, that the objective social importance of the function of the bourgeoisie as a class is not as readily destroyed by its own failure as was true in the case of the nobility. The failing bourgeois family drops out of

the class so swiftly that the class itself always consists of families which are normally equal to their function. Stated in a somewhat different way, with the emphasis on another factor: the nobility *conquered* the material complement to its position, while the bourgeoisie *created* this complement for itself.

The patrimonialization of functional position can always be understood as emerging from administrative expediency rooted in contemporary circumstances. I believe that this applies even to the late Roman version though, especially in our own case, it is but a superficial explanation. Many things that would be socially expedient nevertheless do not happen. Here too the crucial point was severance from a former basic function that was losing survival value—a function that had once been the excuse for active leadership of the whole people. Viewed from this aspect, patrimonialization was the expression of incipient failure, though, from another aspect, it was the consequence and expression of an antecedent success. It reached its peak in those cases where it resulted in the constitution of princely domains—so-called patrimonial states. It is vital to recognize, however, that at bottom such cases are not essentially different from those in which this did not happen—cases of families that for some reason or other never achieved territorial ascendancy. Basically the process was the same, except that certain families simply reached greater prominence than others, and for a long time the dividing line between the two was in a state of flux. It was the same social process, too, that either deprived them altogether of their patrimonialized functional position or (in the few cases in which this did not happen until much later or did not happen at all) created something altogether new, connected with it only by outward forms, associations, and historical continuity—namely, the modern monarchy. At first glance such a conception seems puzzling and in conflict with the facts of legal history, but it immediately loses this character when we add, first, that such cases of outstanding success, though of the same character as the less successful ones, had, in practice, different effects. They created, above all, a special legal form for themselves, emphasizing their unique character and elaborating precisely the consequences of this peculiarity—just as, in an earlier age, the counts had insisted that they were counts rather than knights. Then too, such outstanding success justified the general taking over and vigorous exploitation of all the remaining powers that had once belonged to superordinate authorities. With respect to the development of nonfeudal classes, such powers gained special importance, and they helped those who had won preeminence to consolidate their territorial position—a position that surely represented something new, distinct from the position of other families in the same class; indeed, a position which, under pressure of the new conditions, ceased to function along class lines and actually, as we have seen, turned against the lesser positions of other class members. The picture changes, secondly, when we add that the process by which patrimonial position disintegrated in the face of outstanding dynastic success ran quite differently when success was less sharply marked, precisely because the peak performance ultimately led to a position *sui generis.* The facts in point here are so familiar that we merely have to point out the results that flow from their analysis. Whether by slow pressure or deliberate act, prince as well as landlord was deprived of his patrimonial position by the *same* new structural relations that grew from the successful fulfillment of new functions.

18. Not always, but predominantly—though to a declining degree—the functions involved in the attainment of outstanding success were exercised by members of the nobility.[9] There are many reasons for this. The existing class relationship facilitated mutual understanding and concerted action. By tradition the nobiltiy was fitted for the tasks immediately in hand—quite apart from the traditions of war, there was the lordly mode of life, the habit of command and of handling people, of much greater importance in practical action than mere technical competence; even in our own times many outstanding presidents of English railway companies have been members of the court nobility. To complete the

list of the most important considerations, there was finally the need to keep the nobility occupied, to tie it to the dynasty, to maintain its prestige among the people. This led to powerful customs and taboos which strengthened the position of the nobility all the more, since they perpetuated certain feudal and patrimonial elements which created the illusion of the continued existence of the old system. These customs included the long-maintained practice of reserving high government office to the nobility, the requirement that even ordinary army officers must show descent from a certain number of aristocratic ancestors, and so on. The practices of simony and patronage were specifically patrimonial and in most countries endured deep into the eighteenth century; in the English army, for example, they were abolished only during Gladstone's second ministry. Semi-dynastic succession in office likewise disappeared but slowly. As late as Louis XIV, Colbert and Louvois were succeeded by their sons in the same or similar offices, and the fact attracted not the slightest notice. It is nevertheless important to realize that this function of the nobility, though tending to preserve its position, merely shuffling the position of families, and serving to admit an infusion of new blood (the present-day high aristocracy was largely formed in this fashion), was something altogether different from the former warrior function of the nobility—this, of course, is self-evident—and also different from its position of leadership in public affairs during the Middle Ages. That position was then filled by warlords and by the military class generally, in their own right and with their own resources, regardless of feudal subordination. Now it was exercised at the behest, not of the feudal lord, but of the sovereign, in his borrowed right and power. The core of the system had vanished, its meaning and social content had changed. What did continue, maintaining the position of the nobility, though at a steadily declining rate, were merely accessory elements—ancient prestige, access to and fitness for certain key government jobs and political functions (now superseded by the modern trained expert), intimate contact between class members which facilitated survival, a material basis in agriculture and sometimes industry, stemming from land ownership, incidental opportunities of all kinds which were open to the individual in an "elevated" position. All this, however, tended to be swept away in time. And, confirming our basic view, the process did not take place uniformly and mechanically, but with characteristic differences, according to whether one or the other element of position could be made the basis for social function and success.

19. What we have been discussing is only an example, though one that demonstrates all the important elements essential in answering our question. It shows not only how our thesis may be proved, but also how it is meant to be understood. In particular there now emerges, much more clearly than would be possible from a general discussion, the sense in which we speak of a socially necessary function, of class activity and orientation to activity which we, the observers, understand to be necessary for the survival of the social group, under a given set of circumstances and with a given disposition on the part of the people, and which the group itself senses to be vital for survival. We have only to add the following:

All functions that can be distinguished in the case of a given people and in a given historical situation are "socially necessary." This criterion alone, therefore, cannot decide their relative evaluation. Evidently it is a question of how important the individual class member is in a given situation more particularly, to what degree he can be replaced. The individual warrior in the Middle Ages was less replaceable and individually more "important" than the peasant. The individual industrialist is less replaceable and individually more "important" than the individual worker.

The social importance of class members varies with our two basic elements—the importance of the class function and the degree of success in carrying out that function. But the relation is not always a direct one. Other causes often appear to be far more conspicuous and immediate. Yet such causes, on their part, can always be reduced to those basic elements, just as, according to the economic interpretation of history, the flow of social events is always ultimately shaped by the inner logic of the economic machine, though very often this influence is anything but direct. It is especially the inertia of once solidly established positions that creates a discrepancy between theory and practice, opening up a long chapter of intermediate processes. But these positions themselves can be made comprehensible in accordance with our principle.

Only this latter element explains why the evaluation of a function and the evaluation (that is, the social value) of a class do not always run parallel; why, instead, changes in class evaluation tend to lag behind changes in the evaluation of functions. This also explains the fact that, on first impression, it is more correct to describe the evaluation of a function as dependent on the social rank of those who exercise it. We say, for example, that the social rank of a class depends on the evaluation of its function by the social group, or on its importance for survival, and that "function" often appears at first, not as the prime mover, but as an accessory factor, something quite spearate.[10] And this impression is strengthened—but also fully explained—by still another factor: socially necessary functions are not simply coordinate specialties. They do not all have the same relation to the leadership of social groups. Quite apart from the question of the degree to which *individual* members of the class are replaceable, the *intensity* of this relation to leadership provides a criterion for ranking socially necessary functions above and below one another and not simply for placing them beside each other as mere social necessities. But social leadership can express itself in many different concrete activities, and those which are chosen by a once-dominant group will thereby achieve higher social evaluation.

When we survey the ideas set forth in this section, we see that the causes that account for shifts in the relative positions of classes also, *ipso facto,* account for the original order of rank—the order in which we find them at the outset of any given period. We also see why it is not always easy to establish an unequivocal class hierarchy, why there cannot always be "ruling" classes. More than that, it follows immediately that the same factors which ultimately account for shifts in class position in historical time and for the existing class structure at any given point in time, also answer the question of why there is such a phenomenon as class structure at all. For a class *gains and loses position in the same way that it emerges and passes as a class;* and only because an individual class *does* emerge and pass is there the general problem of class structure.

SUMMARY AND CONCLUSIONS

20. The facts and considerations that have been presented or outlined may be summarized as follows:

Shifts of family position within a class are seen to take place everywhere, without exception. They cannot be explained by the operation of chance, nor by automatic mechanisms relating to outward position, but only as the consequences of the different degree to which families are qualified to solve the problems with which their social environment confronts them.

Class barriers are always, without exception, surmountable and are, in fact, surmounted, by virtue of the same qualifications and modes of behavior that bring about shifts of family position within the class.

The process by which the individual family crosses class barriers is the same process by which the family content of classes is formed in the first instance, and this family content is determined in no other way.

Classes themselves rise and fall according to the nature and success with which they—meaning here, their members —fulfill their characteristic function, and according to the rise and fall in the social significance of this function, or of those functions which the class members are willing and able to accept instead—the relative social significance of a function always being determined by the degree of social leadership which its fulfillment implies or creates.

These circumstances explain the evolution of individual families and the evolution of classes as such. They also explain why social classes exist at all.

We draw the following conclusions from these statements:

The ultimate foundation on which the class phenomenon rests consists of individual differences in aptitude. What is meant is not differences in an absolute sense, but differences in aptitude with respect to those functions which the environment makes "socially necessary"—in our sense—at any given time; and with respect to leadership, along lines that are in keeping with those functions. The differences, moreover, do not relate to the physical individual, but to the clan or family.

Class structure is the ranking of such individual families by their social value in accordance, ultimately, with their differing aptitudes. Actually this is more a matter of social value, once achieved, becoming firmly established. This process of entrenchment and its perpetuation constitutes a special problem that must be specifically explained—at bottom this is the immediate and specific "class problem." Yet even this entrenched position, which endures in group terms, offering the picture of a class made secure above and beyond the individual, ultimately rests on individual differences in aptitude. Entrenched positions, which constitute the class stratification of society, are attained or created by behavior which in turn is conditioned by differential aptitudes.[1]

From other points of view—some of them still in the field of sociology, others beyond it and even beyond the field of science altogether—the essence of social classes may appear in a different light. They may seem organs of society, legal or cultural entities, conspiracies against the rest of the nation. From the explanatory viewpoint they are merely what we have described them to be. And all that is left for us to do is to particularize, illustrate, and supplement our own result in certain points.

21. First, as to aptitude, differences in aptitude, family aptitude: Insofar as "aptitude" is something that shows itself immediately in the physical individual—much like the color of hair or eyes—our line of reasoning, as already indicated, comes back to the physical individual. Insofar as, first, relevant "aptitudes" are not merely physical and, second, "aptitude" can be considered only the basis for "behavior," our argument also comes back to the individual psyche. In our presentation we have endeavored to emphasize that this implies neither the errors of individualism nor a process of "psychologization" that loses itself in surface phenomena. We cannot help those who are unable to see that the individual is a *social* fact, the psychological an *objective* fact, who cannot give up toying with the empty contrasts of the individual *vs.* the social, the subjective *vs.* the objective. But it is more important to guard against tautological confusion between "aptitude" and "success" in which only the latter is taken to be susceptible to empirical observation, while the former becomes a mere word like the *vis soporifica* of opium. We contend that both can be empirically investigated, independently of each other. In the Goths under Teja, we recognize "aptitude" for the function of a military master class, even though history shows that they were not blessed with "success" when they encountered Narses.

To establish the presence of such an "aptitude" does not confer any laurels, nor does it testify to moral worth. From many points of view—religious, esthetic, moral—it may have to be evaluated in a negative sense. It may, in particular, be antisocial—and this is not necessarily a value judgment, but may be a judgment based on facts. Success for the individual, the family, the class does not necessarily mean success for other segments of the population or for the nation as a whole; indeed, it may mean the very opposite. The extent to which this is true is, of course, of considerable importance, not only for our evaluation of the class phenomenon and of certain historical classes, but also for our scientific knowledge of social cause and effect. Even from the examples cited in this study it is evident that in some cases success in establishing class position does represent "social achievement"—in other words, that it enhances the position of others, as well as of those responsible for the success. In other cases this is not true, while in still others the ultimate judgment must depend on a deeper analysis, based on theoretical economics, of the consequences for which the behavior in question is responsible. Finally, a distinction must always be made *between the social significance of a given mode of behavior and the social significance of the qualities that make such behavior possible.* It is not enough merely to have a moral defect in order to become a bandit or a tyrant. As a rule, the person in question must also "have what it takes." In other words, the process of social rise or decline can be described in terms of "natural selection" only in a very restricted sense. But important as these matters are, enlightening as studies concerning them may be, this aspect of the case does not concern us here.

"Aptitude" may be "natural" or acquired. In the latter case it may be acquired individually or by family background. The relevance of these distinctions to our problem is obvious. The greater the role played by natural and family-acquired aptitude, the firmer will class position be. Its firmness will also be inversely proportional to the degree to which an acquired aptitude—of itself or by its effect on the mode and goals of life—prevents the acquisition of other aptitudes, and directly proportional to the degree of significance which outward achievements flowing from an already elevated position carry with respect to the acquisition of new aptitudes. These matters merely have to be mentioned for it to be seen that they hold a good part of class history. But for the first step which our investigation takes they are of no particular importance. Even acquired aptitude is a datum at any given time.

Aptitude determines a quality or a system of qualities only with respect to certain definite functions. The relationship is similar to that between biological adaptation and survival in a given physical environment. There are, for example, specific predispositions—those having to do with music and mathematics have been most exhaustively investigated—which have virtually no relationship to other natural endowments. Yet there are other talents that apply to a multiplicity of functions—the capacity for intellectual analysis, for example. Will power in its various manifestations is an important element in this respect, and there is, of course, the well-known phenomenon of all-around capacity which is equally effective in the face of most of the practical demands of life. Spearman's studies of this quality have given rise to the theory of a "central factor," but actually this is no more than a word for something already empirically confirmed. From the viewpoint of class history and class theory, we are concerned, first, with the fact that class functions and their relative social necessity change only slowly. Secondly, we find that the socially necessary functions that succeed one another in historical time are related in important respects—administrative skill, resoluteness, and the ability to command are vital in any leading position. Thirdly, the functions relevant to our study all have to do with the same factor, namely, social leadership. Over and above this, however, the two cited facts are of the greatest importance to an understanding of class evolution and to any "interpretive" history of class structure. The fact of the special aptitude—especially the acquired kind—emerges with particular clarity when we compare, for example, the type of the warlord of the early Middle Ages with that of the modern stock-exchange speculator. It is a fact that serves to explain why the same class does not always retain leadership—something that is by no means explained by the mere circumstance that the relative importance of functions changes. For the function alone is not the essence of the class. And the facts brought out in the central-factor theory do sometimes explain, in whole or in part, why a class often maintains its social position so well, despite a decline in the function peculiar to it, over a long period of time.

In an ethnically homogeneous environment, special and general aptitudes, physical and mental, those of will and of intellect, are probably distributed according to the normal curve. This has been carefully demonstrated with physical characteristics that are most readily susceptible to measurement, notably body height and weight. Beyond this, we have extensive experimental material only for school children. As for the capacity of adults to measure up to the tasks of daily life, we have only our general impression to go by.[2] Further investigations would be very important in advancing class research, but our present purpose is served well enough by the fact, scarcely disputed, that individual differences in aptitude do exist and that individual aptitudes do not fall into sharply marked categories, separated by empty space, but shade by imperceptible nuances from high to low. The situation is different only when there are sharp ethnical differences, such as between Mongols and Slavs, whites or Arabs and Negroes.

If it were true that individual aptitudes bear no relationship to the aptitudes of ancestors and progeny—if none were inherited and all individuals were simply sports—then the elements of position and acquired aptitude would still be capable of forming relatively stable groups, though the course of history would have been different. If aptitudes were never inherited and always distributed according to the laws of chance, the position of classes and of families within them would manifestly be far less stable than it actually is. There can scarcely be any doubt of the inheritance of physical characteristics. As for mental characteristics, we have as yet only data in the field of defects, though these are in a state of fruitful evolution. For obvious reasons, it is difficult and dangerous to go beyond them, in the field of statistics as well as of genealogy.[3] Again, therefore, we emphasize that while it may be hopeless to pass considered judgment on the cultural significance of a class—and, incidentally, on most other basic questions of the social order, past or future —until this point has been settled, the basic idea of the class theory here presented is quite independent of it.

22. As to the question of leadership, if we are to be properly understood, all the romance and gibberish surrounding this term must be discarded. We are not concerned with the individual leadership of the creative mind or of the genius. We do not care whether this phenomenon is of big or small importance in social science or whether it is irrelevant; whether it plays a causal role, direct or indirect; whether such individuals function autonomously or by their own laws. In short, the entire problem of the "great man" has no bearing on our subject. Nor do we by any means insist that group leadership, which alone concerns us here, necessarily "leads" in the direction where it desires to go of its own free will, or that it creates the realm of possibility into which it leads—a realm realized only under its leadership. We are content to say that social leadership means to decide, to command, to prevail, to advance. As such it is a special function, always clearly discernible in the actions of the individual and within the social whole. It emerges only with respect to ever new individual and social situations and would never exist if individual and national life always ran its course in the same way and by the same routine. Yet by its very nature it almost never occurs in the "pure" state. It is virtually always linked to certain other functions and offices, by virtue of which it is exercised and from which it receives its peculiar coloration and direction. But whatever the trend and the form may be, leadership always remains leadership. Ordinarily individuals differ in their capacity for it, much as they differ in their ability to sing, though it must be added that both the attainment and the practice of leadership are aided by a tradition of leadership. And, as is the case with other aptitudes, the aptitude for leadership is not necessarily strongly marked in a few individuals, and nonexistent in the rest. Most individuals possess it to a modest degree, sufficient for the simplest tasks of everyday life, while one minority has it to a stronger, another to a lesser degree. The absolute extent of aptitude for leadership in a given nation (or the qualities on which it is based) largely determines the history of that nation; and within it indi-

vidual families are ranked by social value in the order in which they possess this aptitude and these qualities. It is because this aptitude is distributed continuously throughout a nation, without gaps and discontinuities, that class barriers are characteristically in a state of flux. Classes particularly deficient or altogether lacking in it secure it through talented individuals who become renegades or declassed. If such classes are already on the rise, they may be led by those of their members who would otherwise ascend to higher classes but instead now devote themselves to the task of leadership within the class. Such ranking by degree of aptitude for leadership is, immediately, one of physical individuals and can owe any supra-individual constancy only to the fact of the inheritance of characteristics. It leads to objectively defined family position and, by extension and entrenchment, to class position of those families that, by our criterion, are approximately coordinate.

23. As for the process of entrenchment, the kind of success that is the basis for the individual's rise normally tends to repeat itself, simply because as a rule the individual manages to carry out the same kind of task again and again and because success generally paves the way for further success. Even so, success, once achieved, exerts a continuing effect, without further accomplishment, for two reasons: First of all, the prestige it engenders assumes a life of its own. It does not necessarily disappear when its basis disappears—nor, for that matter, does its basis readily disappear. *This is the very heart and soul of the independent organic existence of "class."* In the second place, in the vast majority of cases success brings in its wake important functional positions and other powers over material resources. The position of the physical individual becomes entrenched, and with it that of the family. This opens up further opportunities to the family, often to an even greater degree than to the successful individual himself, though these positive factors are to some extent offset by the deadening effect on the original impetus of exalted position and security, by the diversion and complication of interests, and perhaps also by

the sheer exhaustion of energies which everyday experience shows to be not uncommon. *Coordinate families then merge into a social class, welded together by a bond, the substance and effect of which we now understand. This relationship assumes a life of its own and is then able to grant protection and confer prestige.* In addition to the natural endowment of the class members, there are other factors that determine the course and the firmness of class structure and class position—factors that have little or no connection with aptitude. Among those that have no such connection is the outward course of history. There are times of quietude, for example, their tranquillity stemming from causes that have nothing to do with the qualities of the ruling classes, times during which class position is long maintained without effort, times during which only such events occur as the ruling classes are well able to master; and when it is otherwise, events may be entirely beyond control. Another such factor is the character of the economic base of a class. From the viewpoint of the German nobility, for example, it was pure chance that the opportunity existed for large-scale agricultural production which proved to be a very durable and relatively easily managed source of capitalist income. Thirdly, it may likewise be mostly chance, for better or for worse, whether a suitable new function can be found at the time the old one enters into a decline. But this already passes into the other group of factors. It does have some slight connection with the capacities of the families in the class—whether, for example, the class propagates itself or withers by inbreeding. The connection with class aptitude is somewhat closer—whether or not the attainable function is a suitable basis for general leadership. The warlord was automatically the leader of his people in virtually every respect. The modern industrialist is anything but such a leader. And this explains a great deal about the stability of the former's position and the instability of the latter's. Even closer is the connection between class efficiency and adaptability to altered circumstances. There is the aristocrat, for example, who hurls himself into an election campaign as his ancestors rode into battle; and there is the aristocrat who says to himself: "I can't very well ask my valet to vote for me." Here, in fact, is the measure of two radically different types of European aristocrat. The class situation may so specialize members of the class that adaptation to new situations becomes all but impossible. From the viewpoint of this and similar factors, we can see in proper perspective why members of the ruling classes in present-day Europe so often seem to make a bad joke of our theory that class position and capacity go together. Finally, there is but a slight connection between the endowment of a class and the facility with which it grasps and handles growing power. Highly competent classes are often quite blind to the vital importance of this factor, for themselves as well as for the destiny of their people. Yet that importance is unmistakable. It is the ease with which English industrial families in the nineteenth century managed to rise into "society," by way of financial success and politics,[4] that gave England its unique leadership class. This, after all, was true even of rising intellectual talent—and the life stories of two "physical individuals," Disraeli and Lassalle, give symbolic expression to a segment of two national destinies.

NOTES

THE PROBLEM

[1] The author proposes to devote another study to the latter topic. Still another study by the author, *Die Krise des Steuerstaats* (Graz, 1918), seeks to approach the problem of the *Zeitgeist* from another angle. The discussion of economic problems in the present study is necessarily held to relatively brief length and is to be supplemented by a study of neo-mercantilism, yet to be published. Another study, *Die Ideenseele des Sozialismus,* likewise as yet unpublished, is to deal with a related complex of ideas.

IMPERIALISM AS A CATCH PHRASE

[1] To be sure, there were accomplishments in various fields. Above all, the currency was restored. It is also true that coming events were casting their shadows before them—in Huskisson's tariff policy. But overall orientation with respect to the great questions of the day was purely negative.

[2] We shall revert to this point repeatedly in the following.

[3] It is true that certain other acts of Disraeli's could be adduced. But the Zulu War was really the act of the local commander, Sir Bartle Frere, who earned a reprimand from the cabinet. The annexation of the Transvaal (1877), revoked only by the Treaty of London (1884) under Gladstone, was the result of a very

difficult situation vis-à-vis the natives. The Afghanistan adventure, likewise reversed by Gladstone, was a countermove to a Russian advance. And the title of "Empress of India" was a gesture that serves to demonstrate to the hilt the verbal character of this imperialism.

⁴ Egypt was Gladstone's conquest, but a conquest against his will. From the very outset it was intended to leave Egypt to Turkey, and negotiations on this point reached a stage where it was solely Turkey's fault that this intention was not realized. Even so, there was no annexation, though such action would have been diplomatically quite feasible and would even have met the approval of Germany. Later on the situation changed, first because of the gathering agitation among the Mohammedan population and later because of the general worsening of world conditions.

⁵ It scarcely seems worth while still to discuss the stock phrase about "commercial jealousy," which has now been pretty generally abandoned. It has been shown rather conclusively, first, that there were no grounds for such sentiments, and second, that they played a part—and a relatively unsuccessful one at that—only in one segment of the press. This is shown by the very fact that the free-trade policy continued. We shall, however, come upon this question in another context.

⁶ Of course this is not meant to imply that political developments on the domestic scene in any country are somehow dependent on the "fortunes of war." The result of these battles was a natural reflection of social circumstances, especially the relative security from external enemies which placed the crown at a disadvantage in developing its instruments of power. The sentences that follow must likewise be read with this in mind.

⁷ Was, then, the policy of Lord North in accordance with public opinion? No, but he took a beating too. Even in this instance, by the way, the crown had to have a majority in Parliament behind its policies. It obtained this majority by means of corruption. In the end even this method failed whenever crown policy departed too far from the will of the masses. Even the great aristocratic coteries could not in the long run survive without popular favor. As early as the middle of the eighteenth century, that favor was powerful enough to prevail over the crown and the aristocracy, as the career of the elder Pitt shows. It was also powerful enough to make the position of a minister untenable, even though he was the king's favorite, as is shown by Bute's misfortunes.

⁸ A policy that would have been in accord with the past as well as the future was represented by Fox, whose position was weak in Parliament, but relatively strong outside. The mere fact that

such an opposition policy could exist supports the argument of
the text.

⁹ The Holy Alliance resembled a cartel. It was, to be sure, a cartel
of imperialist interests, but by nature it was directed toward
conservation rather than aggression.

¹⁰ The outstanding monument of this policy is Russell's note of
October 27, 1860, in which he backed Piedmont against Naples
and the Pope, in a tone that was then quite unusual in diplomacy. From the "objective" point of view, the Crimean war was
a betrayal of this policy, but "subjectively" it appears in the
light of a defensive war against imperialism.

¹¹ Characteristically, it was Cobden, the leader in the struggle for
free trade, who first successfully represented this policy in public. In his treatise on Russia (1840) he opposed the literary
exponent of interventionism at the time, David Urquhart
(founder of the magazine *Portfolio* in 1835 and author of,
among other works, *Turkey and Its Resources; England, France,
Russia and Turkey;* and *Sultan Mahmud and Mehemet Ali*).
What happened paralleled the fate of every point argued by
utilitarianism and the Manchester school. Both trends were so
unpopular in England, accorded so little with popular inclination, that every politician who desired to get ahead and play a
role of importance, carefully eschewed them. Yet in different
verbal guise one of their points after another was usurped and
realized. The most conspicuous milestone in this process was
Gladstone's speech in the *Don Pacifico* debate of 1850.

¹² On the pacifist character of English foreign policy in the time
prior to the first world war, see Reventlow, *Deutschlands
auswärtige Politik,* 1st ed., *passim.*

IMPERIALISM IN PRACTICE

¹ The psychological aspect here resembles the case of the modern
captain of industry, whose actions likewise cannot be viewed as
a balancing of hedonist purpose against effort which is expe-
rienced as disagreeable. See my *Theory of Economic Development.*

² This is no mere analogy of the kind rightly held in contempt.
We are dealing with the fact that every purposive organization
by its mere existence adapts its members to its purpose.

³ This applies also to the Turkish wars, waged mainly by
Catholic nations. These wars were not crusades and though
the religious element often emerges in them, it never appears
as the motivation.

⁴ In later times Mohammedanism also knew expansion by means

of conversion, notably in India and among the Mongols. But this does not change our diagnosis of Arab imperialism.

IMPERIALISM IN THE MODERN ABSOLUTE MONARCHY

[1] To the need for action there was added the fighting instinct. Royal policy gave direction to both. A mass of subsidiary motives were also present, among which lust for booty, murder, and destruction was by no means absent.

[2] Thus he never carried further Leibniz's plan for the conquest of Egypt. Conquests in the western part of the North African coast would have been even more plausible, but were never considered. Warfare in the colonies was conducted with considerable lassitude and financed only meagerly.

IMPERIALISM AND CAPITALISM

[1] This is not meant to prejudice the question of whether such efforts, in the final reckoning, achieved objective cultural gains or not, a subject falling outside our present province. Personally, I take a predominantly negative view of their significance. But my arguments along these lines are again beyond the present study.

[2] Imperialism is one of many examples of the important fact, already illuded to in the beginning, that the application of the economic interpretation of history holds out no hope of reducing the cultural data of a given period to the relations of production of that same period. This always serves to support objections to the basic economic approach, particularly since one of the consequences of the cited fact is that relations of production in a given period may often be reduced to existing economic sentiments that are independent of those relations. For example, the constitutional and political order of the Normans in southern Italy cannot be explained by the relations of production prevailing in that country. The very economy of the Normans in southern Italy becomes comprehensible only by reference to their capacity and wishes. But this does not actually refute the economic interpretation, for the mentality of the Normans was not something that existed outside the economic sphere. Its sources are found in the economic background from which the Normans came to southern Italy.

[3] There is here a conflict (not elaborated in the present study)

with Marxism, primarily with the theories of increasing misery and the reserve army, but indirectly also with the basic conception of the whole process of capitalist production and accumulation.

⁴ See in this connection especially Lederer, "Zum sozialpsychischen Habitus der Gegenwart," *Archiv für Sozialwissenschaft und Sozialpolitik,* Vol. 44.

⁵ This parallelism, of course, cannot be traced in every individual case. Countries and ideas differ far too greatly for that. Kant, for example, certainly did not have a pronounced capitalist background, though English influences did play an important part with him. His case, by the way, offers the occasion to point out that we mean our assertions to apply to *all* types formed by capitalism, not merely, or primarily, to capitalistic classes in the sense of *propertied* classes—in other words *the* capitalist class. A misunderstanding in this respect would be regrettable. It should be further emphasized that utilitarianism was not a philosophy of capitalists, either by origin or social tendency, although it was a *capitalistic* philosophy in the sense that it was possible only in a world of capitalism. Indeed, the "capitalist class" in England preponderantly and sharply rejected utilitarianism, from its early beginnings to its culmination in the younger Mill, and so did the big landowners. This fact is commonly ignored, because utilitarianism fits in so well with bourgeois practice. It does so, however, only so long as its distorted journalistic projection is confounded with its true character, only when it is taken at face value. Actually it shows an unmistakable kinship to socialism, in its philosophic approach, its social orientation, and many of its practical demands. It is the product of capitalist development, but by no means of capitalist *interests*. Pacifism, for example, can be shown to flow from it—though not from it alone. Present-day pacifist tendencies have their roots largely elsewhere, notably in Christian thought, which, of course, preceded the capitalist era, though it could become effective in this direction only in the capitalist world. Unfortunately it is not possible here to set forth these things at length and thus to guard our views against the danger of being misunderstood.

⁶ It is an interesting fact, by the way, that while the peace policy is certainly not rooted in the capitalist upper class, some of the most eminent exponents of the political interests of the trusts are among the most zealous promoters of the peace movement.

⁷ Rather, imperialist and nationalist literature is always complaining vociferously about the debility, the undignified will to peace, the petty commercial spirit, and so on, of the capitalist world. This in itself means very little, but it is worth mention-

ing as confirming a state of affairs that can be established from other indications.

[8] The stubborn power of old prejudices is shown by the fact that even today the demand for the acquisition of colonies is justified by the argument that they are necessary to supply the demand for food and raw materials and to absorb the energies of a vigorous, rising nation, seeking world outlets. Since the flow of food and raw materials from abroad is only impeded by tariffs at home, the justification has no rhyme or reason even in our world of high protective tariffs, especially since in the event of war traffic with colonies is subject to the same perils as traffic with independent countries. For the rest, the element of war danger circumscribes what has been said in the text to the extent that it creates an interest in the control of such food and raw material producing countries as are situated so as to offer secure access even in wartime. *In the case of universal free trade, however, the danger of war would be substantially less.* It is in this sense that the sentence about dominion of the seas, which follows in the text, must be understood.

[9] Even with free trade there would be capital exports to the countries offering the highest interest rate at any given time. But that flow would be lacking in any aggressive character, just as would be true of export of commodities, which would be regulated by the law of costs, or, if capital and labor were but incompletely mobile, by the law of comparative costs. Any forcing of exports, whether of commodities or of capital, would be senseless.

[10] Workers too may be temporarily placed in dire straits by a shift to other industries or methods that becomes necessary in such a case. For some individuals a shift to occupations for which they are not qualified may be altogether impossible. As a class, however, and in the long run, workers only gain through such a process—unless the industries forced out of business by competition employ relatively more workers than those which proceed to occupy the places made vacant. For in general, under free trade, production opportunities are better exploited, greater quantities are produced, and, all other things being equal, more workers are employed too. To be sure, these "other things" are by no means always equal, but that does not change the core of the argument. The fear that domestic industry will be undersold by the foreign products of cheaper labor and that wages will be consequently depressed stems from popular superstition. Actually such a danger exists to but a trifling degree. But we cannot deal with all of these questions here.

[11] Capitalism is its own undoing but in a sense different from that

implied by Marx. Society is bound to grow beyond capitalism, but this will be because the achievements of capitalism are likely to make it superfluous, not because its internal contradictions are likely to make its continuance impossible. This is not properly part of our subject. I do wish, however, to preclude any interpretation that I regard capitalism as the *final* phase of social evolution, as something that exists of natural necessity, that cannot be adequately explained. Still less do I regard it as an ideal in any sense. I do not go along with Hilferding, incidentally, in anticipating that trustification will bring about a stabilization of capitalism.

¹² The reasons may, in part, lie in the fact that orthodox socialism has always been inclined to regard the question of protective tariff *vs.* free trade as something of essential concern only to the bourgeoisie, something almost unworthy of socialist attention, to be left to literary polemicists who are in the habit of compromising with the existing order. Tactically this attitude can scarcely be maintained any longer today, nor *is* it maintained with respect to export monopolism. Yet it was tactically comprehensible in Marx's own time, for any other stand would have compelled him to admit a community of interests between the proletariat and the contemporary bourgeoisie— in England an interest in free trade, in Germany an interest in an "educational tariff," which he and Engels acknowledged. The stand, however, did impair theoretical understanding. It was one of the elements in the incorrect total evaluation of the effects of the system of free competition: especially of what Marx called the "anarchy of production," but also of the suicidal stimulus of profit, and finally, of the movement toward concentration. What was indirectly at stake was the entire concept underlying the theory of underconsumption, impoverishment, and collapse. Adherence to these views, regarded as essential to "scientific socialism," has led to far too favorable an evaluation of export monopolism, which is supposed to have brought "order" into "anarchy." See Lederer's excellent study: "Von der Wissenschaft zur Utopie," *Archiv für die Geschichte des Sozialismus und der Arbeiterbewegung,* Vol. VII.

¹³ An imperialism in which the entrepreneurs and other elements woo the workers by means of social welfare concessions which appear to depend on the success of export monopolism may be called "social imperialism," a term appropriate to the factual situation, but certainly not implying imperialism on the part of the working class. Social imperialism in the sense of an imperialism rooted in the working class does not exist, though agitation may, of course, succeed in kindling such a mood locally and temporarily in the working class. Social imperialism in the

sense of imperialist interests on the part of the workers, interests to which an imperialist attitude ought to correspond, if the workers only understood it correctly—such an imperialist policy oriented toward working-class interests is nonsensical. *A people's imperialism is today an impossibility.*

14 Methodologically, it is interesting to note here that, though nationalism and militarism are not "reflexes" of the capitalist alignment of interests, neither did they emerge as what they are today during the periods in which they had their roots. Yet they do not necessarily escape the focus of the economic interpretation of history. They are the forms assumed in the environment of the modern world by habits of emotion and action that originally arose under primitive conditions.

THE PROBLEM OF CLASSES

1 We also mean to imply that a class is no mere "resultant phenomenon," [*Resultatenerscheinung*] such as a market, for example (for the same viewpoint, from another theoretical orientation, see Spann, *loc. cit.*). We are not concerned with this here, however. What does matter is the distinction between the real social phenomenon and the scientific construct.

2 In support of this criterion we may now also invoke the authority of Max Weber, who mentions it in his sociology, though only in passing.

3 We do not use the term "estate" since we have no need of it. Technically it has fixed meaning only in the sense of status and in connection with the constitution of the feudal state. For the rest, it is equated, sometimes with "profession," and sometimes with "class." Caste is merely a special elaboration of the class phenomenon, its peculiarity of no essential importance to us.

4 The theory of the "original" classless society is probably headed for a fate similar to that which has already overtaken the theory of primitive communism and primitive promiscuity. It will prove to be purely speculative, along the line of "natural law." Yet all such conceptions do receive apparent confirmation in the conditions of the "primitive horde." Where a group is very small and its existence precarious, the situation necessarily has the aspects of classlessness, communism, and promiscuity. But this no more constitutes an organizational principle than the fact that an otherwise carnivorous species will become vegetarian when no meat is available constitutes a vegetarian principle.

5 The explanatory value of historically observable genesis must

not be overrated. It does not always lead to an explanation and never offers an explanation *ipso facto,* not even when a phenomenon appears immediately in its "pure" form, which is neither inevitable nor even frequent.

THE RISE AND FALL OF FAMILIES
WITHIN A CLASS

[1] With blood relationship the critical factor, we do not limit ourselves to the parental family here. Hence we use the terms family, clan, tribe as synonymous, though a presentation that went into greater detail would have to make distinctions.

[2] More precisely: independent of positional elements that are recognizable before the event occurs. For the event may be—and generally is—tied to some one of these elements.

[3] Such aggressiveness was a mode of life, important to the knightly estate as a method of natural selection. In the case cited this is seen—if evidence be needed—from the events following the capture, twice in succession, of Aggstein, robber citadel of the Kuenringens, each time by captains of the regional prince. Each time the captor, duly invested with his prize, was aping his predecessors in a matter of months.

[4] I refer to my exposition of this mechanism in my *Theory of Economic Development,* which devotes a special chapter to it, though the topic is also discussed elsewhere in that treatise.

[5] These cases, however, include those that are "historically" most significant and thus widely known to the public. The rule is control by a syndicate or an even weaker organizational form.

[6] This is an important factor of success and social ascent in every walk of life. It is what the English gambler calls "playing to the score."

MOVEMENT ACROSS CLASS LINES

[1] The monarchial position is not something *sui generis,* but simply the topmost position of the high aristocracy as a class—even though, in the individual case, the monarch may hold quite aloof from that class.

[2] See Sir J. Stamp's communication in *The Economic Journal,* December 1926.

[3] *Cf.* Chapman and Marquis in the *Journal of the Royal Statistical Society,* February 1912.

[4] Both the fact of class struggle and the expression itself would

then appear in a different light; but it is important to emphasize that they would not lose all significance.

THE RISE AND FALL OF WHOLE CLASSES

[1] Of course it is by no means a matter of indifference whether failure acts in this fashion or objectively and automatically, as in the case of a businessman, for example. But these finer distinctions, essential to an interpretation of class history, cannot be considered here.

[2] Specialization along occupational lines need not, of itself, tend to form classes. Men and women have always had distinct spheres of work, yet they never formed "classes" on the basis of mere inter-individual relationships.

[3] Legal and social history usually treats this rise from the opposite aspect—the decline in the position of other elements in the population.

[4] True, this process was not completed until the twelfth century. Earlier techniques of war did not impose even approximately such demands, as has already been indicated. Yet while acknowledging the importance of this element, it must not be overestimated, even for later times. The equestrian art in our sense, or anything like it, did not even exist before the time of the classical school. There were then no assemblages of armored horse, no training in cavalry techniques.

[5] The Saxon nobility colonized East Elbia in the same way and at about the same time as the Byzantine nobility colonized the southern and eastern border reaches of Asia Minor.

[6] I employ this term, suggestive of the economic interpretation of history, in order to give expression to my belief that our line of reasoning is entirely reconcilable with that approach.

[7] Incorrectly because there is implied a distinction between the spheres of private and public law, which is peculiar only to the age of capitalism. But we are here concerned only with characterizing a familiar phenomenon.

[8] They do not do so at the same rate, however, as is shown by the examples of the English and French aristocracies. Sharp breaks in constitutional continuity and excesses are only symptoms of *revolution,* just as panics and depressions are symptoms of economic *crisis;* but the essential thing is a process of transformation that *may* but *need not* lead to revolution or crisis. The position of classes is not won or lost, in a causal sense, through revolutions. As Gottfried Kunwald puts it: when one already *has* the power, one can make a revolution, among *other*

things; but power that does not exist cannot be *created* by revolution.

[9] To the extent that other persons were involved, they were "elevated" and assimilated to the nobility—not always voluntarily.

[10] It is more accurate, by the way, to say that class determines "occupation" than the other way round.

SUMMARY AND CONCLUSIONS

[1] It is only this process of entrenchment that creates a special cultural background, a greater or lesser degree of promptness in concerted action, one aspect of which is expressed in the concept of the class struggle. We refrain here from passing any judgment on the actual significance of this factor.

[2] The impression is not entirely a general one, for we do have concrete instances to go by, notably studies of relatively homogeneous bodies of civil servants.

[3] This becomes clear in its full significance when we compare Goddard's study of the Kallikak family, for example, with Galton's *Hereditary Genius*. But both material and methods are steadily improving. Even today, we can agree that K. Pearson's pithy statement, "ability runs in stocks," is far truer than its opposite, especially since everyday experience confirms it. But should not then class position, once established, endure *ad infinitum* in every case? Before we embarked on our study, this might have been a reasonable question. But I have no answer for those who put it at this point.

[4] A noteworthy feature of this system is the elaborate "ordeal" which the rising family as a rule had to endure.

A SHORT BIBLIOGRAPHY

WORKS BY J. A. SCHUMPETER

The Theory of Economic Development. Cambridge, Harvard University Press, 1935.

> Schumpeter's most important work. It contains the first and most explicit statement of his theory of capitalist dynamics.

Business Cycles: A Theoretical, Historical and Statistical Analysis of the Capitalist Process, New York, McGraw-Hill, 1939.

> A restatement and critical examination and testing of the main theories contained in *Theory of Economic Development.* A book of profound historical and theoretical erudition and learning.

Capitalism, Socialism and Democracy, New York, Harper & Bros., 1942.

> An examination of the forces in modern society and, simultaneously, an evaluation of socialist and capitalist alternatives to social organization.

Wesen und Hauptinhalt der theoretischen Nationalokönomie, Leipzig, Duncker & Humblot, 1908.

> Schumpeter's first book. A skilful analysis of the main theories of economic analysis and an examination of the nature of partial and general equilibrium analysis in economics.

Essays, edited by R. V. Clemens, Cambridge, Addison-Wesley Press, 1951.

A collection of Schumpeter's economic essays mostly from his Harvard period.

Ten Great Economists from Marx to Keynes. Oxford University Press, New York, 1951.

Ten biographical essays written at various times during Schumpeter's life. These essays exhibit at the same time Schumpeter's skill as a biographer and his sharp wit in evaluating the theories of his peers.

The History of Economic Analysis, edited by Elizabeth B. Schumpeter, New York, Oxford University Press, 1954.

Probably the most extensive and most complete analysis of the history of economic thought. This book is destined to remain for long a landmark in its field.

Economic Doctrine and Method, edited and translated by R. Aris, London, Allen & Unwin, 1954.

A translation of one of Schumpeter's early works in German. A short and lucid account of the history of economic theory omitting many of the specialized topics treated in the *History of Economic Analysis.*

WORKS ABOUT J. A. SCHUMPETER

The Schumpeterian System. By R. V. Clemence and F. S. Doody, Cambridge, Addison-Wesley Press, 1951.

A critical exposition of Schumpeter's economic theories in a systematic form.

Schumpeter, Social Scientist, edited by Seymour E. Harris, Cambridge, Harvard University Press, 1951.

Twenty essays by different authors on the life and on the various aspects of the work of J. A. Schumpeter.

Joseph A. Schumpeter

Joseph A. Schumpeter was born in Triesch, Austria in 1883. After a European career divided among business, teaching, and active politics, he spent the last twenty years of his life until his death, in February 1950, as Professor of Economics at Harvard. Among his works are: THE THEORY OF ECONOMIC DEVELOPMENT; BUSINESS CYCLES; CAPITALISM, SOCIALISM, AND DEMOCRACY; and THE HISTORY OF ECONOMIC ANALYSIS.